I0759674

‘In our worrying world and busy lives, faced by constant challenges of work, money, health, relationships, confidence and responsibility, how difficult it is to hear that "still small voice of God" that we know brings calm and comfort. This intuitive, beautifully-written book offers gentle company along the bumpy road of day-to-day life, reminding us that God never lets us stray from the palm of His hand, and that His love is unconditional and forever.’
Pam Rhodes, English television, radio presenter and author

‘In *Beloved Is Where We Begin*, Rachael crafts a clear pathway through mental and spiritual uncertainty, reminding us that divine love persists even when our capacity to feel it falters. This deeply personal journey through the liturgical year offers gentle, accessible wisdom for the overwhelmed and weary – you could call it a sanctuary in book form that beautifully demonstrates how our belovedness is not something we earn, but the very foundation from which all healing begins.’
Revd Dr Cris Rogers, author of *Making Disciples* (Lion Hudson, 2018)

‘This gentle, accessible devotional speaks love and truth in every breath. I felt encouraged, nurtured and loved as I read its words. Far from a superficial read, however, I was equally challenged by insights which exposed where my thoughts and feelings had diverted from God's best. I recommend *Beloved* for all!’
Lucy Rycroft, author and founder of thehopefilledfamily.com

‘This book is a wonderful liturgical walk through the year, with gently hopeful reminders of our belovedness and beautiful original prayers and blessings. For anyone feeling ashamed, broken or overwhelmed, this book is pure balm.’
Tanya Marlow, author of *Those Who Wait* (Malcolm Down, 2017)

‘*Beloved Is Where We Begin* is a book that will be beloved by many. It's a life-giving devotional full of Godly encouragement from a deeply authentic author. In its weekly meditations, you'll be invited to soak in your beloved identity as a believer – through every season of life – whilst being reminded that we are most missionally impactful when we're most secure in God's magnificent love. It's full of the healing balm of God's grace that binds up our bruised and broken hearts, and its breath prayers and blessings are beautiful.’
Howard and Holly Satterthwaite, speakers, coaches and authors of *Spiritual Detox* (SPCK, 2021)

‘This is a gift of a book, so generously crafted and gifted to us by Rachael. To say that we're God's "beloved" is easy, it's central to our faith. But to live it? Now, that's hard. To truly believe such a thing – on our worst days as well as our best days – it can feel painfully difficult. And that's why this book is such a gift. It aids us in dwelling on the truth, giving the love of God the space and time to sink into our bones once more. It's a tender companion, a gentle friend, the wisest company. It's a book that I needed more than I knew.’
Dr Belle Tindall, journalist, presenter and author of *Witch Hunt* (SPCK, 2026)

‘Rich with blessing and prayer. Resonate with an honesty of life lived and love known. Rachael Newham invites us to fifty-two weeks of wondrous work, of "liturgy", as together we seek to understand the breadth and depth of God's love for each of us. Truly, beloved is where we begin.’
Revd Canon Rob Merchant, Dean of Mission, Ministry & Education, Diocese of Chelmsford

Rachael Newham is an author and speaker specialising in the theology of mental health and illness. She founded the Christian mental health charity ThinkTwice while at university, and after completing her research masters looking at a pastoral theology of depression, she led it for a decade. Rachael has also held roles at several national Christian charities working to change the conversation around mental health. She now writes, speaks and consults on issues of mental health and faith on a freelance basis. Her first two books, *Learning to Breathe* and *And Yet*, are also published by SPCK. She lives in Hertfordshire with her husband and young son, and can be found with a coffee in hand among her colour-coordinated bookshelves. You can find her on social media @RachaelNewham90 and substack.

For my son Sebastian, who teaches me about loving and being loved every day.

First published in Great Britain in 2025

Form
SPCK Group
Studio 101
The Record Hall
16–16A Baldwin's Gardens
London EC1N 7RJ
www.spckpublishing.co.uk

British Library Cataloguing-in-Publication Data
A catalogue record for this book is available from the British Library

ISBN 978-0-281-09111-9
eBook ISBN 978-0-281-09110-2

1 3 5 7 9 10 8 6 4 2

Typeset by Fakenham Prepress Solutions
First printed in Great Britain by Clays Ltd

eBook by Fakenham Prepress Solutions

Produced on paper from sustainable sources

BELOVED IS WHERE WE BEGIN

A weekly devotional for sustainable rhythms of grace

Rachael Newham

Contents

Introduction

It was the kind of spring day that makes photographers of us all. I was in the bucolic setting of the Retreat House at Pleshey. The blossom was blooming and wildflowers waved gently in the breeze.

As I looked at my surroundings, I felt a strange mixture of peace and anguish; peace because I was with a team I loved, doing a job I felt confident in, but anguish because I was grappling with the mental illness that had recently re-taken the driving seat of my life. I was as sure as I'd ever been about my faith in God, but as far as I'd ever been from feeling the hope, love, joy and peace I believed in.

I wrote furiously in my journal, finding as I had before that my thoughts took on texture and sense as I inscribed them on the page. My eyes surveyed the beauty around me and I felt the following words settle in my heart: 'Beloved is where we begin.'[1]

I'd read the phrase in a book of blessings a few months before and it had stayed in my mind ever since. But at that moment I felt the alchemy of faith when the words moved from my head to my heart. It chimed with everything I'd experienced of the Christian faith in the decades since I first believed: that even when everything else shifts, when doubts cloud my thinking, and despair consumes my joy and vitality, I am never able to shake the knowledge that we have all been created and loved by our Father God who crafted the cosmos.

It's often said that preachers end up preparing the sermons they most need to hear. I don't think that's ever rung as true as while I've been writing the book in your hands. In the years the ideas in this book have been percolating, and the months in which I've written them, I've never needed more to hear about the love God has for us.

I've needed it as I've ridden the rocky waves of a mental illness that seems to have taken on a life of its own. I've needed it as my husband and I have navigated parenting with my increasing disability. I've needed to be reminded, over and again, that being beloved is not something we earn, not something that decreases with our productivity.

Our 'belovedness' flows straight from the heart of our Creator who, despite knowing the possibility of horror that it could result in, decided to give us the choice to love him rather than create automatons.

I wrote this book not just for my own eyes, however. I wrote it for those unable to sit through a sermon because they're shushing babies in the back row; for those whose physical and mental torment make traditional church difficult for those who spend their Sundays rushing between serving on multiple teams or preaching to their own congregations.

I hope and pray that if having a daily quiet time has become an impossibility, for whatever reason, or is rushed through while brushing your teeth, you can carve out twenty minutes just once a week to be still and tune your heart to the still, small voice of the Lord. Ideally, you'll be able to read the whole passage suggested each week, but if energy or time restricts you, I've included the key verse at the start of each chapter.

If there is anything that stays with you from these pages, I pray it is that you are beloved by God and there is nothing that can take it away from you or separate you from it. Beloved is where we begin – and our belovedness will lead us home.

I've written this book in fifty-two chapters that can be read weekly, each ending with a prayer or blessing you can carry into the rest of life. It's designed to follow the liturgical year through the seasons of Epiphany, Ordinary Time, Lent, Easter, Pentecost, a second period of Ordinary Time and ending our calendar year with the beginning of the liturgical year in Advent.

The word 'liturgy' can feel far from daily reality for some of us, but in practice it simply means 'work of the people'. It reflects how God speaks to us through all we do. By following the liturgical year, we get to experience the life, death and resurrection of Jesus, with their associated emotions, together as a community. Sometimes these seasons will chime with seasons in our own lives; at other times they will be in stark contrast. We might grieve through Christmases and experience great joy in times of corporate lament like Lent.

We're beginning in January, as that's when most of us like to start new year-long devotionals. Because of this, the weeks may not quite align with the dates of Lent, Easter and Pentecost every year, as Easter is always the first Sunday after the full moon on or after the spring equinox in Britain, so it is quite literally a moveable feast. Feel free to skip to the Lent chapters so you can read them in real time, then catch up on any missed weeks later in the year.

Some of the entries in this book end with blessings, some with portions of Scripture to pray. Others finish with breath prayers. Breath prayers are designed to calm your nervous system as you speak to God. The inhale breath is shorter (as is the corresponding phrase) and the exhale breath is longer to allow for the nervous system to regulate. As Lesley Alderman writes in the *New York Times*:

> Consciously changing the way you breathe appears to send a signal to the brain to adjust the parasympathetic branch of the nervous system, which can slow heart rate and digestion and promote feelings of calm as well as the sympathetic system, which controls the release of stress hormones like cortisol.[2]

The way our breathing can calm our emotions is a beautiful reminder of the intricate way God designed each and every one of us to live, to cope with hard times and to remember that we are loved by our Creator with an everlasting love.

I hope this is a book you can return to when loss and the clamour of life have drowned out the knowledge that you are loved. I pray that you may drink again from the Scriptures and be reminded of what never ceases to be true, the words written in the letter to the church in Ephesus all those millennia ago:

And may you have the power to understand, as all God's people should, how wide, how long, how high, and how deep his love is. May you experience the love of Christ, though it is too great to understand fully. Then you will be made complete with all the fullness of life and power that comes from God. (Ephesians 3:18–19, NLTUK)

Week 1
Third Sunday of Christmas/ New Year

Reading: Isaiah 43:16–21

> See, I am doing a new thing! Now it springs up; do you not perceive it? I am making a way in the wilderness and streams in the wasteland.
> (v. 19)

It's all over the magazines, websites and social media. The beginning of a new year is a time ripe for reinvention. There seems to be a media clarion call of 'New Year, New You' whether or not that is wanted, needed or indeed helpful.

Conversely, this time of newness is also a time of reminiscence. As we approach something new, it may be human nature that compels us to look back at what has been. I know that as a new year begins, I can get so caught up in the Instagram round-ups and Year in Review, it is tempting to miss the excitement and hope of what is to come.

This is what I think is happening in this passage that at first glance seems somewhat contradictory. We have Isaiah recounting the way in which God saved the Israelites from Pharaoh by parting the Red Sea, before telling them, 'Forget the former things; do not dwell on the past' (v. 18). But this is not a universal call to dismiss everything God has done for them. It is a reminder that his work is not all in the past; it is current and dynamic. God was not finished with them – and he isn't finished with us.

I can sometimes be tempted only to reflect on what God has done in my life and not consider what he might do. I can sometimes think that the best days are perhaps in the past. I wonder if you do the same?

But there is hope. And this passage encourages us to find the balance between our gratitude for what God has done and our hope for what is to come. Isaiah begins by describing what God has done for them, before moving on to what God is promising to do for them in future.

They are to be thankful that in the past God parted the seas and they are to anticipate that God is going to make 'streams in the wasteland'. It is not the case that God has finished working – there is more to the story of their redemption. And there is more to our story of redemption.

Jesus lived as a human and struggled as we do. He died and rose again for our sakes. He ascended to glory, but that wasn't the end. He will return to make everything new, and all the pain of humanity that he himself suffered will be soothed, and every tear wiped away.

The promise of the new heaven and new earth is proof that God has not finished with us. He is working among us now through his Spirit and we will one day join him in the new earth, where there will be no more sin and no more mourning.

As this new year begins, let us hold fast to God's unchanging, unshakeable promise to be with us and to remain with us in loving-kindness until the very end – whatever this coming year has in store for us.

Blessing

A new year has fallen like snow.
And like the snow it may cover what has gone before but it won't erase it.
Last year might have been one of tribulation and triumph.
Perhaps it was a year of survival.
Perhaps survival was the triumph.
You may not quite be ready to be grateful for the year that has gone,

But we may be grateful for the people who have walked these days alongside us,
Those who will cross the threshold.
Do not be afraid to celebrate if yours was a year of wins.
Do not be afraid to grieve if yours was a year of losses.
We can co-exist in our losses and gains, our gratitude and our grief;
Weeping with those who weep and rejoicing with those who rejoice.

Week 2
Epiphany

Reading: Matthew 2:1–12

> On coming to the house, they saw the child with his mother Mary, and they bowed down and worshipped him. Then they opened their treasures and presented him with gifts of gold, frankincense and myrrh.
> (v. 11)

Right here at the start of our calendar year, the season of Epiphany begins. It's marked on 6 January each year and invites us to understand that Jesus came, not just to be 'God with us' but also to show us the glory of God, and that the two cannot be separated. Jesus' humble entrance into time and space cannot be extrapolated from his glory as the Son of God available and accessible to even those most unexpected.

The story of the wise men is familiar, re-told in nativity scenes and school plays a thousand times over. We are used to hearing of the wise men guided by the star to see Jesus, bearing the gifts of gold, frankincense and myrrh. And yet what is superficially about offerings to the infant Jesus is deeper and darker than we might wish to imagine.

We have assumed there to be three wise men because there were three gifts, but Matthew never tells us how many of them there were. All we know is that they travelled first to King Herod, to the palace where they expected to find this new king. As the late Timothy Keller notes, they were words no king would have wanted to hear: 'Now when you come into a palace and ask, "Where is the king?" it is going to alarm the person actually sitting on the throne.'[3] King Herod was 'disturbed' by the wise men's quest for a king, and what it meant for him. There was surely no room for two kings on his throne.

The first manifestation of Jesus to the wise men is one full of beauty and significance; the gifts foreshadow Jesus' life and death to come, with the gold fit for a king, frankincense for worship and myrrh to anoint the body that would die for us all. But the latter is all the more disturbing, for it continues to show us that Jesus will be a king like no other. In his youngest years, he became a refugee fleeing Israel, after Joseph was warned in a dream of King Herod's murderous intentions.

If the birth in a manger was an inauspicious start, becoming a refugee was even more so. There was a sign even then that following Jesus was not going to be for the faint-hearted, as Herod ordered the slaughter of infant boys under the age of two, to try to eradicate the threat this new king posed to his own rule.

Right from the very beginning, we are shown that the arrival of Jesus, with his gifts of majesty, was not divorced from human pain. God did not send Jesus to be set apart from the reality of the human condition, but to experience it fully. Even as we take the Christmas decorations down at Epiphany – or before if we cannot resist cleaning our home on 1 January – we are reminded that Jesus came into a moment in history steeped in horrors similar to our own.

By not turning away from the horror of Herod amid the joy of the wise men's visit, we are shown that there is not a shade of human life untouched by the love of God.

Blessing

He came in the dark
To people unexpected,
To welcome the wounded
And the wandering.

They were guided in the dark
By stars unlike any other.

They brought gifts of darkness,
The shining gold for a king.

Born into obscurity
The fragrance of frankincense
Welcoming us into holiness.
The myrrh preparing
A baby for his death.

He came for the mighty and meek.
He came like stars
Piercing our darkness,
Lighting our way, hope against hope
Until the stars burst and kingdom comes.

Week 3
First Sunday of Epiphany: Jesus' baptism

Reading: Matthew 3:13–17

> And a voice from heaven said, 'This is my Son, whom I love; with him I am well pleased.'
> (v. 17)

If any story in Scripture tells of our beginnings in belovedness, it is this one. It's a story about who Jesus is and why he came in perhaps the plainest terms available.

My own baptism was one I'd eagerly anticipated since the age of five when I became a Christian at my church's holiday club. It was then I decided I wanted to go all in and be baptised as a believer too. I wanted it so much that I asked every year until I was thirteen and our new minister finally said yes!

Unsurprisingly, I had no in-depth theology of baptism at the age of five (or in the years that came afterwards), but I was aware that it was about telling everyone I knew that I loved Jesus and wanted to follow him through whatever life would throw my way. I think my levels of excitement about my baptism were perhaps only matched a decade later in the run-up to my wedding! I was fulfilling a dream I'd had for most of my conscious life. I knew even then that my future lay in Christian ministry and this felt like the beginning.

When I went into the waters, however, it wasn't excitement that overwhelmed me; it was peace and what I can only describe as assurance. I had felt the love of God so powerfully when I'd said yes to following Jesus aged five and I felt it again in that moment. But I also understood, perhaps for the first time, that the journey I was embarking on wasn't going to be easy.

Following Jesus isn't easy. It doesn't guarantee happiness or ease (however much the prosperity preachers might like us to believe that), but it offers the assurance of God's presence and love through whatever we face.

Jesus' own baptism affirms this in ways I didn't appreciate at thirteen, for he descended into the waters of baptism, not to be cleansed from sin like we do when we're baptised, but to ensure he fully entered into the human experience. Jesus' baptism was him taking, as one commentator notes, 'the first step on the road to Calvary'.[4] Even the act of asking his cousin John to baptise him demonstrates his humility in being willing to fully enter into humanity, and we know that afterwards he would go into the desert and be tempted with all the power of heaven that he gave up to be 'God with us'.

Above all, though, the baptism of Jesus is a reminder that being loved by God comes before anything else. Before the miracles and the work of Jesus Christ, before he had walked the path to the cross and beyond, the Father reminded him of who he was and whose he was in Matthew 3:16: 'This is my Son, whom I love; with him I am well pleased.'

They are words from the Father to his Son, but I also believe they are a reminder to us that, whatever other names we will receive over the course of our lives, we are first and foremost children of God, lavished in love before we even lift a finger. As 1 John 3:1 proclaims so powerfully: 'See what great love the Father has lavished on us, that we should be called children of God!'

I have needed reminding of this in my life more times than I can count. Particularly when I've become mired in all I cannot do; in all the ways I fail to live up to my own standards. And perhaps you feel the same way too?

The reminder is right here: it is not what we do that makes us lovable; it is how we begin. It is because of this love that we can do anything at all.

Below is a prayer/poem. Read it through a few times and ask the Lord to let the truth of your belovedness settle into your heart and be the power that fuels you in the week to come.

Blessing

Was the water warm to touch?
Or did it cool his sun-soaked skin?
Did he take his bewildered friend
By the hand as he asked for baptism?

A cleansing for the sinless one
Welcomed to the family he made.
Was the water clear?
What could be seen?

As he dove into the waters
And emerged from them again,
All that mattered was his name,
Beloved by God, pleasing to him.

He knew the path that lay ahead

Like us he knew the start for all:
Beloved is where we begin.

Week 4
Second Sunday of Epiphany: Water into wine

Reading: John 2:1–11

> What Jesus did here in Cana of Galilee was the first of the signs through which he revealed his glory; and his disciples believed in him.
> (v. 11)

As miracles go, turning water into wine isn't one that would be considered high on the priority list. In comparison with what would come later, where demons were driven out and life was snatched from death's clutches, Jesus' first miracle can seem curious – extravagant, even.

And yet this first miracle reveals something beautiful about the character of God. It tells us that God is not just concerned with the big things, but with every detail of our lives. In this case, running out of wine would have been a social embarrassment for the hosts of the wedding.

The setting of this first miracle is important, though, because marriage in the Jewish context represented the coming together of God with his bride – his people. Jesus undertook this first miracle in Galilee, which had a large Gentile population. This is a sign that Jesus came to share the love and generosity of God beyond the walls of the Temple – with the whole world.

This first miracle was also done at the request of Jesus' mother, Mary. When the wine had been used up, Mary approached Jesus and told him of their predicament. At first glance, Jesus' response was perhaps less than compassionate. John 2:4 documents him saying: 'Woman, why do you involve me? … My hour has not yet come.' It's perhaps not the kind of response we'd expect from Jesus. But despite his seeming lack of enthusiasm, he directed the servants to fill the jars with water and present them to the banquet master.

It's the first sign in the Gospel of John of the new creation that Jesus' coming was heralding. The signs include the feeding of the five thousand, walking on water and the resurrection of Lazarus – all of which are evidence that the coming of Jesus was the beginning of a new creation of the whole world and for the whole world.

These signs show us not only the power of God, but the lavish generosity of God. The miracle could have just been that Jesus quietly replenished the wine that had been used up. Typically the lower quality wine was reserved for the guests to consume once the best wine had dampened their tastebuds. Instead, the wine that Jesus created from the water was of the best quality. It was radical and extravagant generosity and a testimony to us about the character of the God we serve. As author Rachel Held Evans has commented: 'The 150-plus gallons of wine at Cana point to a generous God, a God who never runs out of holy things.'[5]

So often the God we hold in our imagination is stern, someone we don't associate with fun or levity; but the generosity of God in this story demonstrates the beauty at the heart of the character of God.

In a world that encourages us to count every penny given away, and to ensure that every hour is billed, the generosity of Jesus is counter-cultural. He didn't just save the hosts from the disgrace that would have arisen if they'd run out of wine at the wedding. He presented the best when everyone would have expected the worst.

The generosity of Jesus is a hallmark of his love. It was generosity that threw a lavish party for the prodigal son who returned home, when he only expected the job of a servant. And generosity that saw the shepherd risk everything, abandoning the ninety-nine to rescue the lone lost sheep.

If we are to be people rooted in the love of God, then we are to be people of radical generosity. This isn't just with our material things, but with our love, in our patience with the people in front of us in the queue, with our kindness and in our perseverance when things are hard. These characteristics can become so much a part of us that we cannot be distinguished from them.

Breath prayer

Inhale: God of generosity
Exhale: Let us share your love

Week 5
Third Sunday of Epiphany: First disciples

Reading: Mark 1:16–20

At once they left their nets and followed him.
(v. 18)

I gave one of my first sermons on this passage. Yet as I was re-reading it to prepare to write today, I was struck by something I'd never noticed before: Jesus didn't need disciples. He didn't need a team to work with. He was there at the creation of the universe! But Jesus chose teamwork. He chose to be surrounded by followers, not because he needed them, but because we need to follow him. The disciples demonstrate for us the reality of following Jesus in a way that I'm not sure we could have understood in any other manner.

Immediately before this passage, Jesus had begun to preach: 'The Kingdom of God has come near. Repent and believe the good news' (v. 15). In Mark's telling, there is no preamble; the first preaching of the good news demanded that it was shared. We are told immediately that sharing the good news is not a solo mission.

Jesus technically didn't need a team to work with – he's the Son of God who does miracles – and yet he chose to do this work of salvation alongside friends. The disciples were chosen for no other reason than because he wanted humanity to be a part of his saving work.

It's the same from the beginning of time. God chose to do in collaboration with humanity work that he could have done alone.

God chose to give Adam and Eve a role in the care of creation, and here again Jesus decided to give ordinary men and women a role in his mission.

But Jesus didn't have the kind of recruitment process we might expect. In fact, he didn't seem to have a process at all. He called those he passed, asking them to follow him without ever really giving them an idea about who they would be following and what it would entail. He included as his disciples hated tax collectors like Matthew, and lowly fishermen, but for all of them it was a call they could not refuse. Mark tells us that as soon as Jesus called, James and John left the boat and their father immediately. They didn't spend time weighing up options or deliberating about which path to take. The disciples seem to have followed Jesus without a second thought for what they were leaving behind. I can't help but wonder why, and what my response would have been. I'm almost certain that I wouldn't have left everything I was familiar with in any haste – I'm indecisive enough about the most trivial decisions in life! But Jesus' words, 'Follow me', aren't just reserved for his disciples; they're for all of us. In fact, they're repeated some twenty times in the gospels alone, encouraging us that it is a call open and available to everyone, both then and now.

What the call to follow shows us about Jesus is that we are not promised perfection but rather presence. The disciples did not become immune to suffering when they followed Jesus (quite the opposite), but they never had to face the troubles of the world alone. They had one another, but more importantly they had Jesus. He was with them through the times when I wonder if they regretted their decision. They found themselves in conflict with the religious leaders of the day and questioned their master's choices as he ate with social outcasts and allowed himself to be touched by the ritually unclean.

The disciples were not the perfect followers; most abandoned him when the going got tough. But, for the most part, they continued in the call to follow him even once he'd ascended to heaven as they received the gift of the Spirit and began the work of the earliest churches.

They are proof that following Jesus is not about our own qualities and strengths, but about the power of God's love, which fuels and fires our journey on the path set before us. We are not promised tranquillity, but transformation and the presence of the Spirit of God through whatever we may face.

Blessing

We can only see our next few steps.
We cannot know how the path
Twists, turns and changes.
We can only know the name
Bestowed upon our hearts
Before they hit a single beat.
Beloved.
Our belovedness does not
Straighten our paths.
It promises that
Through every danger,
Toil and snare
We will be led
By amazing grace,
Unfathomable love,
Shalom.

Week 6
Fourth Sunday of Epiphany: Candlemas

Reading: Luke 2:22–39

> Coming up to them at that very moment, she gave thanks to God and spoke about the child to all who were looking forward to the redemption of Jerusalem.
> (v. 38)

Candlemas reminds us that the arrival of Jesus is not the start of a brand-new story, but rather a new chapter in a continuing story. It places him in the Jewish tradition, and the life ahead of him in the light of the prophets who spoke of their Messiah. It's a mixed message for Mary; one of triumph and trouble from Anna and Simeon, whom commentators describe as 'Israel in miniature'[6] and who had waited their whole lives to see the promised Messiah.

Candlemas demonstrates Mary presenting Jesus at the Temple in accordance with Jewish law, but also bringing the significance of Jesus and his saving work to those outside the Jewish faith. It expands the scope of Jesus' saving grace to all of humanity.

Anna and Simeon represent the hope and warnings of the Old Testament prophets, and the messages they had for Mary and Joseph were not the common messages of congratulations that new parents often expect to hear (although they may have cooed over how cute the baby Jesus was too … we will never know!). Instead, they told the story of the struggle and suffering Jesus would endure and the promise he would bring.

The Lord had promised Simeon that he would not die until he had seen the Messiah, so the account is rich with anticipation. When he held the infant Jesus, he spoke the powerfully prophetic words in this passage, which describe not only Israel rising and falling, but state that 'a sword will pierce your own soul too'. It's not the kind of message a new parent wants to hear, but it was one full of truth; for the life of Jesus would hurt Mary in ways even his miraculous birth could never prepare her for. The name Simeon is derived from a word that means 'to hear intelligently'.[7] It is exactly what he did, not just listening to the message he wanted God to bring but being faithful to the truth of God's word, even when it wasn't particularly happy – a reminder perhaps that the good news is not necessarily happy news.

Simeon is the only person in Scripture we hear of holding the infant Jesus other than his parents. In his arms, the reality of Jesus' identity and future was revealed. Where Simeon left off, Anna picked up.

Anna's testimony was to everyone who was 'looking forward to the redemption of Jerusalem'. Where Simeon explained the warning Jesus would bring and the sword that would pierce Mary's soul, Anna's message was one of comfort that Jesus was to be the Saviour of the whole world. Despite meeting him at only a few weeks old and despite her advancing years, she went on to spread the good news.

Like many Christian festivals, Candlemas was originally a pagan celebration. It was the time Imbolc (St Bridgid's Day) marked the midway point between the winter solstice (the shortest day of the year) and the spring equinox. It was the beginning of the lambing season, signified by the lighting of fires. The celebration of Candlemas was chosen to coincide with this date.

Celebrating Candlemas reminds us that the coming of Jesus is the coming of the light of the whole dark world.

Breath prayer

Inhale: The world is dark
Exhale: Jesus is the light of the world

Week 7
Third Sunday before Lent: Tapestry of life

Reading: Ecclesiastes 3:1–8

> There is a time for everything, and a season for every activity under the heavens.
> (v. 1)

Just a few weeks into the new calendar year and we've reached the first period of the liturgical year called Ordinary Time. 'Ordinary' here refers to 'ordinal' (first, second, third and so on) rather than 'not special', and these two periods follow a season of celebration leading up to a time of preparation, each week named with the ordinal followed by 'before' or 'after' (as here, for example, Third Sunday before Lent).

Despite this technical explanation of Ordinary Time, I can't help but think that there is something to be said about God speaking to us throughout the year – not just during the seasons and celebrations that have the most prominence in the Christian calendar. So much of our lives is 'ordinary' (in the 'routine' sense of the word): the commute, the school run, making meals, organising appointments. These things make up most of our lives, even though it's often the dramatic or difficult parts that we remember most. Through all of this, despite what our days may consist of, we remain loved by God.

Rhythms are built into our DNA. They were established at creation itself. In Genesis 1:5 we read, 'And there was evening, and there was morning – the first day.' Each day is organised to have both darkness and light, morning and evening, and the liturgical year gives us a chance to see this on a bigger scale as we journey through the darkness and light of the ancient stories that form our life and faith.

The author of Ecclesiastes is unknown, but is often referred to as Qohelet, or teacher. The teacher asserts that life is fleeting, and cycles through grief and joy, rough waters and smooth, but also encourages us that life has space for all these seasons, and the liturgical year does too. 'There is … a time to be born and a time to die … a time to weep and a time to laugh.' The verses highlight the extremes and demonstrate that every season, whether that be the life cycle, our emotions or our communal states, is not only a part of life but it will be made beautiful.

This doesn't mean that war is beautiful or that tears are a part of God's great plan for his creation. But it does mean that, in our fallen world, they are inevitable and one day all that is painful and ugly will be made beautiful, whether that be later in life or when the world is made new.

Life is often likened to a tapestry, where on one side there is a mess of different-coloured threads that seems disorganised and unattractive. Yet on the flip side there is a beautiful image that depicts something meaningful. You and I can confidently await the day when the mess in our lives is revealed to have been woven into the story of God's creation and made impossibly beautiful. Arguably the messier one side of the tapestry is, the more beautiful the other side.

In human life, we will experience the full spectrum of emotions and life. There's no doubt about it. What Ecclesiastes tells us is that basing our lives on the ebb and flow of our experiences and emotions will leave us empty. We need something greater, something more meaningful than the things that will change on a dime.

Ecclesiastes reflects the spirit of Ordinary Time. It shows that God is interested in and a part of every detail of our lives and world. There is nothing too big or too small in the course of our lives that God does not care about. It's one of the greatest wonders of the love of God that the same God who crafted the stars is interested in the minutiae of our lives, our commutes and communities, daily chores and the tiny interactions we have with one another.

Prayer

Take a moment now to pray through Ecclesiastes 3:1–11, asking God to be tangibly present and active in each part.

Week 8
Second Sunday before Lent: Defined as beloved

Reading: Genesis 1:1–27

> So God created mankind in his own image, in the image of God he created them; male and female he created them. (v. 27)

Sometimes I worry that we skip a vital part of the biblical narrative. We think that the story of humanity begins with the Fall, with the snake and the disastrous consequences that provide an explanation for the chaos and calamity we are so familiar with in our world.

We can get so caught up in whether the account of Genesis 1 is the literal way the earth was formed, questioning where the dinosaurs fit into the story (well, that's my son's main concern anyway), that we neglect the most beautiful message of the beginning of Scripture. I recall studying the arguments for creation at school, using the analogy of the intricacy of a clock that proved there was a creator. But even such technical excellence cannot come close to the intricacies of creation in which ecosystems and processes come together. We see even the smallest, and perhaps most annoying, creatures like flies work together to enable creation to flourish and roll through the cycles of life and death.

The point of the creation narrative in Genesis 1 is not to explain the scientific minutiae of how creation came about. It's to show the unfolding story of God's relationship with humanity, seeking to answer why a timeless, limitless God chose to create a world full of beauty with the potential for such terror.

The first chapter in the first book of Scripture gives us the answer: it was for God's delight. When God created, by turning on the lights right through to the crafting of humans, the reaction was one of pleasure: 'God saw that the light was good' (v. 3).

And, as he continued, he proclaimed everything that he created to be 'good', until he formed humanity and called us 'very good'. This is where our story begins, not with the tragedy of the Fall and exile from Eden, but with the fact that goodness is the hallmark of creation. Author Lisa Sharon Harper says: 'The original hearers and readers of Genesis 1 would have understood that the writers were not merely saying that each part of God's creation was very good but rather that God's mighty web of interconnected relationships was forcefully good, vehemently good, abundantly good!'[8]

The Genesis story contrasts starkly with the other creation narratives of the Ancient Near Eastern period, which feature warring gods and creation emerging incidentally from destruction. Instead, we have a story of our Creator deliberately and intricately crafting something out of nothing, bringing order out of disorder, and God's created beings loved and wanted from the beginning.

Belovedness is our heritage and the hope that will carry us. It is in our DNA and comes before any other identity. We are loved because God chose to make us and proclaimed our goodness, and the goodness of all creation, at the moment of making.

We know what happened to creation. We know of the Fall that changed everything and opened the doors to the pain and disconnection it ushered in when Eden was sealed off from us. What we cannot forget is that our roots are not in our sin. We were not made for evil, but for goodness, and our name will never cease to be Beloved. Our story is one of God seeking us out and drawing us close to him whenever we wander away.

We cannot escape our brokenness. We see it all too clearly on display through environments that crumble, relationships that rupture and wars that rumble. But neither can we escape our belovedness. It was there in the beginning and follows us all the days of our life. As author Brennan Manning says: 'Define yourself radically as one beloved by God. This is the true self. Every other identity is illusion.'[9]

Breath prayer

Inhale: Thank you for loving me
Exhale: May beloved be my identity

Week 9
Sunday before Lent: Clothed in mercy

Reading: Genesis 3

> The Lord God made garments of skin for Adam and his wife and clothed them.
> (v. 21)

The passage recounted in Genesis 3 is often called 'The fall of humankind'. It details how the serpent began his temptation of Adam and Eve by questioning the rules God had handed down to them. It's a story we are probably familiar with: the origin of sin and brokenness and how it came to be in our world.

And yet there is a detail that I think too often gets lost and missed in the retelling. While humanity's faults and failings are key points in the narrative, I can't help but be drawn to the actions of God amid the mess left by sin. There are undoubtedly clear consequences, but there is also a demonstration of mighty mercy towards Adam and Eve: the clothing of their nakedness.

It's a detail that gets lost in the unveiling of their sin and the listing of the consequences of that sin which take up much of Genesis 3. But it's one that reminds us that God's care for Adam and Eve, and indeed the whole of creation, doesn't end with their sin.

The sign of that first sin is not the nakedness itself. The bodies God has given us do not become inherently sinful. It's Adam and Eve's awareness of their nakedness. They suddenly had the knowledge they were never meant to have. I wonder, as I write, if that's because God knew full well what awareness of our bodies would do to our minds. Perhaps he knew how we would become obsessed with perceived imperfections and unable to be satisfied with what God had provided for us.

We see a glimpse of how we were meant to inhabit our bodies when we see children smiling at their reflections. Showing my son his reflection was an almost fail-safe way to get him to smile when he was a baby, such was the joy that his reflection brought him! He still shows that delight today, yet as he grows older, I know that what has been a source of joy may not always remain so. It is our job as his parents to ensure that his happiness is not rooted in his reflection.

God's response to our sin, and the subsequent awareness of our nakedness, is not to change our bodies. He does not declare that our bodies are now bad, but he does recognise that our sin has brought shame, and he covers it for us. The animal skins demonstrate the sacrifice required to pay for our sins. They foreshadow the sacrifices people would be required to give to come close to God, be they ritual sacrifices or the passover lamb. They point forward to the sacrifice Jesus would make once and for all on the cross at Calvary.

God doesn't take the blame for us as if he's a character in a soap opera who has lied for his children only for it to haunt him years later. God's forgiveness wipes us clean and allows us to be reconciled to him, first through the animal sacrifices offered at the altar and finally at the cross.

God's forgiveness of Adam and Eve didn't mean they were exempt from the consequences of their sin. They still had to leave Eden. But they were allowed to build a life after paradise. They went on to have children and establish a home. They were no longer untouched by sin, but neither were they immune to God's blessing.

The sin of humanity doesn't mean we are excluded from the love of God. It means that love and mercy cover us and allow us to continue to approach the throne of grace, not cowed, but confident. Later, in the gospels, Jesus tells the story of the prodigal son and shows us that despite our sins we are still welcomed by the Father. Luke 15:22–24 says:

> But the father said to his servants, 'Quick! Bring the best robe and put it on him. Put a ring on his finger and sandals on his feet. Bring the fattened calf and kill it. Let's have a feast and celebrate. For this son of mine was dead and is alive again; he was lost and is found.' So they began to celebrate.

In the same way that Adam and Eve were covered with animal skins, the prodigal son was covered with the best, and celebrated. This was not because of his sin, but because of his return home. Our reconciliation relies on the loving-kindness of God, not our own righteousness.

Breath prayer

Inhale: For God so loved the world
Exhale: That he sent his one and only Son

Week 10
First Sunday of Lent/ Ash Wednesday

Reading: Joel 2:12–17

> Rend your heart and not your garments. Return to the Lord your God, for he is gracious and compassionate, slow to anger and abounding in love, and he relents from sending calamity. (v. 13)

Lent is a strange time. There is dust and darkness, repentance and weeping, with strange trepidation for events that are both ancient and thoroughly present. Ashes are, as the author Stephanie Duncan Smith says, 'the anointing no one ever asked for'.[10] We know that Easter will come, but it feels far off.

I have found myself feeling strangely comfortable in Lent. There is a reality and a grounding nature to it. Perhaps it's because I recognise the wrongness in myself and my own life. But I struggle to put words and feelings to the wonders of the resurrection that I know the dark days lead to. For so many of us who live with chronic illness, loneliness and many other unnamed griefs, Lent does not feel limited to the forty days; it feels like the state in which we live permanently.

In some ways, I try to approach Lent as if I don't know the ending. I find we all too easily skip past these days to the pastel-coloured celebrations of the glorious resurrection. But there is time for that. Aren't we told in Ecclesiastes 3:1, 'There is a time for everything, and a season for every activity under the heavens'?

And this is a time of coming back to God; from the pushy advertisement of all life's comforts for our pain to the slower, often harder but more beautiful, work of God. Joel 2:13 invites us to: 'Rend your heart and not your garments. Return to the LORD your God, for he is gracious and compassionate, slow to anger and abounding in love, and he relents from sending calamity.' Break your hearts, Joel is telling people. Break your hearts for all that is wrong in your lives and the world around you and return to God, who is waiting not with a shaking fist or fire of damnation but with grace and compassion.

Gideon Heugh[11] helpfully reminded me on his Instagram of the Greek and Hebrew words we translate as 'repent': the Hebrew *t'shuvah* and the Greek *metanoia*. Respectively they mean 'to return' and 'to change one's mind'. This Lent I want to invite you on a journey that may well see your heart break, because there is so much in this world and in our own lives that hurts more deeply than our hearts can bear.

But more importantly, I want us to remember the invitation to return to God, however long it's been and whatever mess accompanies us. Our Father is waiting open-armed with his love and compassion. It's the picture painted by Jesus in the parable of the prodigal son found in Luke 15, in which the son asked for his inheritance early, wasted it on a life of debauchery and found himself feeding pigs and being so hungry he envied them their pig food! At that point he decided to return to his father's house and offer to be a paid servant. Instead, his father greeted him with lavish love and forgiveness: 'But while he was still a long way off, his father saw him and was filled with compassion for him; he ran to his son, threw his arms around him and kissed him.'

We may feel a long way off, far from home, far from hope, far from the people we want to be and the God we long to love again, but God hasn't stopped waiting for our return. His abundant love is not far off. It waits for us with comfort for our broken hearts, and wisdom for our future unimagined. It is an unshakeable love that is ours if we can just allow ourselves to change our minds and return to our Father.

Blessing

Bury your hallelujah.
Remember your finitude.
But never forget you remain as beloved now
as the day God reached into the dust, crafted humanity –
and called it very good.
The ashes remind us of inseparable truths: we're made from dust, we will return to dust
and yet God formed every beloved atom of us from that dust
and sent his Son to return to dust because of his great love for us.
We are further from Eden than we can bear but we remain his beloved creation,
and the ashes from last year's palm-crosses powerfully remind us of that.
It is easy, too easy, to see the brokenness in and around us;
it is marked on our hearts in the way the ashes mark our foreheads today.
But it cannot and will not quench our belovedness.
It is where we begin – even this journey.

Week 11
Second Sunday of Lent: That's my boy

Reading: Matthew 17:1–11

> While he was still speaking, a bright cloud covered them, and a voice from the cloud said, 'This is my Son, whom I love; with him I am well pleased. Listen to him!'
> (v. 5)

I have spent much of my life being comforted by Jesus' humanity: his pain and longing, the way he drew close to the suffering and the small. It has, I guess, been my life's message. And yet what I am sometimes prone to forget is that the power which created stars and crafted landscapes was from Jesus. As John writes in his gospel, 'He was with God in the beginning' (John 1:2). And I think that perhaps this strange story of Jesus' transfiguration is included as a reminder of the mystery of Jesus' immanence and transcendence, woven together in a way that cannot be undone. As the late great Eugene Peterson said: 'What it took John a long discourse to recount is here brought together in a picture so that we can see it all at once: God is present. His dwelling is with humankind in power and glory.'[12]

There is more to this story though. As I've read it and studied it, I've seen an aspect that I entirely missed before. I knew it was a turning point in Jesus' ministry, as he set his face towards Golgotha and all that was coming for him. He was being shown as the Messiah, blazing between Elijah and Moses and revealed as greater than them both. But what I didn't consider was this verse where the voice of God speaks from the heavens. *The Message* translates

Matthew 17:5 as: 'This is my Son, marked by my love, focus of my delight. Listen to him.' Alongside the glory, alongside the miraculous sight of the heroes of Israel appearing beside him, is the voice of the Father. Abba declaring his love for Jesus as his Son. It seems to meet a very human need that we all have: the approval and love of a parent before we embark on a new phase of life or work. I know I need the comfort and encouragement of my parents still!

We are seeing again, as we did at his baptism, that the first words God has for Jesus are of love and approval – and they echo through the ages to us. Simon Ponsonby says:

> Jewish hope and belief was that when the Messiah came, God's cloud of glory would return. And here it is – here God is, here the king is. And the voice of God speaks, just as it spoke in the beginning… The Father says 'That's my boy'.[13]

'That's my boy' is a phrase that speaks of the best closeness, pride and friendship that fatherhood, and parenthood, can offer. And these were God's words for his Son before he began the hardest period of eternity, where he would suffer unspeakable pain and die so that we too may be called beloved sons and daughters of God.

They are words for us as we face unspeakable pain and pressure, or delight, in life. It is our belovedness that led Jesus to the cross – and it is out of belovedness that we were created and will be led home again.

Blessing

There is more loss than we can bear,
More fear than we feel we can conquer.
There is more darkness within and around,
More hatred than our hearts can acknowledge.
And yet light still breaks through at dawn,
Beauty still graces our brokenness.
So I will perhaps foolishly trust
That love can still stand,
That hope can still survive,
That faith can still sustain.

Week 12
Third Sunday of Lent: Living water

Reading: John 4:1–26

> The woman said, 'I know that Messiah' (called Christ) 'is coming. When he comes, he will explain everything to us.' (v. 25)

I don't know about you, but I don't think I'd be all that happy if someone listed everything I'd ever done, including every way I'd been hurt and every way I'd hurt myself and others. And yet here is this unnamed Samaritan woman rejoicing because of just that – Jesus knew her and all she'd been through. Jesus' knowledge of her was enough for her to know that he was the Messiah. Again we see Jesus being revealed in ways and through people we would least expect.

I should probably rewind a little, as you may not be familiar with the story of the woman at the well from chapter 4 of John's Gospel. Much has been written about this woman, but she met Jesus precisely because she didn't want to be seen or known. She went to draw water from the well in the heat of the day just so that she could be alone and avoid the crowds. In general, people drew their water in the morning when it was coolest. This was a time for community and catching up with friends. But this Samaritan woman didn't want that; she wanted the solitude, and was prepared to face the discomfort of the hottest part of the day. It's what shame does, isn't it? It forces us into painful places so that we can avoid being seen. It makes this trade-off seem worth it.

Jesus, however, cut through this woman's shame-fuelled desire to hide away and spoke straight to her. What makes it more remarkable is that this woman was a Samaritan, and Jews (and Jesus was one) would not usually have anything to do with them. It was a divide as old as time. By asking her to draw water from the well, Jesus was showing us that the Messiah is for everyone – even the most hated.

This woman would have been hated even in her own community. The reason she'd been visiting the well alone was because she'd been married several times and the man she was living with wasn't her husband. For Jesus to accept water from her would have made him ritually unclean – and yet his love saw past that to bring her to himself.

Traditionally she has been blamed for her circumstances and considered immoral or promiscuous. And yet, as Elaine Storkey points out, 'In a patriarchal culture, women could not divorce their husbands; husbands divorced their wives.'[14] So her divorces were not of her doing – she had effectively been abandoned by several men and she was paying the price of shame for her pain.

This is often still the case today, sadly. We experience great pain and then are shamed for it, feeling the need to keep it a secret, whether that be for a broken relationship, living with the stigma of mental illness, needing to receive benefits or any other pains that come with added and unnecessary shame.

Jesus met a woman who was fearing hate with a love that would change her life, and later in the passage we read that many people came to Jesus because of her testimony. When Jesus declared that he knew everything she'd ever done, he was opening the floodgates of his love and salvation to everyone.

Jesus' living water is there to wash all of it away and refresh our wounded hearts, bodies and minds. That's for everyone, no exceptions. I don't know about you, but I need that living water as much today as the woman at the well did thousands of years ago. I need the refreshment, the healing and the hope that living water brings, and our breaking and broken world needs to hear about it. So perhaps, for us, it's not about telling everyone everything we've ever done, but about showing and telling everyone what Jesus has done out of love for us.

Breath prayer

Inhale: Lord of mercy
Exhale: Meet us in our mess

Week 13
Fourth Sunday of Lent/ Mothering Sunday

Reading: Exodus 2:1–10

> When the child grew older, she took him to Pharaoh's daughter and he became her son. She named him Moses, saying, 'I drew him out of the water.'
> (v. 10)

The story of Moses' birth and early years is some tale, isn't it? And yet I think we often neglect the fact that this story is one of mothering. It's not our traditional idea of mothering, but the wider and more beautiful vision of mothering we see in Scripture. The word 'mother' may be a tender wound for some – for those who are longing to be mothers, those grieving their children or mothers, or for those whose relationship with their mothers is far more complicated than they can explain. But as we look at the three very different versions of mothering we see in Moses' story, I hope that you take comfort in the idea that mothering is a verb that we can partake in, not just a person we encounter.

First, there is Jochebed, Moses' birth mother, who, as Kelley Nikondeha describes, 'birthed life under a death order',[15] as many mothers in wartime do across the world. There is such tenderness in how Jochebed's mothering is described: she hid him because he was a 'fine child'. Now, while it's common for parents to think their child is the most beautiful baby ever to be born, the language here links us back to the creation story. The word we have translated as 'fine' (*tov*) is the same word God uses to announce that his creation is 'good'. The material of the basket she put her son in made it an ark of sorts, lined with tar to keep it afloat. We're meant to see the parallels between Moses' trip down the Nile and Noah's ark, which carried God's faithful through the flood.

Jochebed's mothering used the force that Pharaoh wanted to use to kill her baby to save him. Does it remind you of another story where the power of death is used to save life? Mothering is a reflection of God's heart just as much as fathering is. It's the power of love and life over the forces of evil and death.

As Jochebed sent her baby boy along the river in the hope of saving his life, Moses' big sister, who we will later learn was called Miriam, kept watch. I love this image of a small girl watching over her baby brother as he floats along the Nile, mothering him from a distance and then stepping in to ensure that her own mother can remain a part of his life. Miriam fought for Moses in her mothering, and her role in this story, arranging for her mother to be paid for nursing her child, allowed them to remain close. It is proof, if ever we needed it, that the role of mother includes those who advocate and care for life just as much as when they generate life.

And it's here that we meet Moses' third mother figure: the pharaoh's daughter, Bithiah. She was born into unimaginable privilege and was presumably well aware of the grief her father's policy was unleashing on the Hebrew people.

Bithiah is an example to us all of how to use our privilege. I expect it was a risk to take in this baby, but various Bible translations talk about her being moved with compassion. She allowed herself to be led by her love rather than her fear, in the same way that Jochebed and Miriam did before her.

Protection is an inescapable part of mothering. Whether it's mums protecting toddlers from scaling heights, or the fight to make streets safer for women to walk, it's another reflection of the God who loves and protects with tar-lined baskets and nails in a cross to save us from a death without him. And when Bithiah drew the infant from the water, she too was playing her part in God's salvation plan.

The work of mothering is the work of God; it's a reflection of the love of God for his family that welcomes everyone. It seats the sinners and the saints together to share in the body and blood of Christ. As women all over the world pour themselves out for their children and in their communities, we can catch a glimpse of our God whose power parted the Dead Sea and whose love reached down from heaven to rescue each one of us.

Blessing

Through his Spirit, may God bless those longing for their mum this morning.
May he comfort those who grieve for what was, or what could have been.
May those who long for motherhood be cradled by God's love,
And may all who gather at this table share in the body and blood of God's Son,
And be met with the joy of belonging together in God's family.

Week 14

Fifth Sunday of Lent: Jesus wept

Reading: John 11:1–44

Jesus wept.
(v. 35)

It's the shortest verse in the Bible and, perhaps strangely, it is my favourite. For me, it encompasses all that is precious and unique about the Christian faith. For while all other gods strive to display their 'otherness', our God sent his Son into humanity, not just to save it but to be a part of it, to be incarnate and experience the agony of humanity for himself.

It is astounding to me, even now as I write about this passage for probably the fiftieth time, that the one who was there when the stars were made became one of us and wept with us. As Black Liturgies writer Cole Arthur Riley says: 'You can't tell me that it doesn't change everything that the one who created all things and holds together all things, cried.'[16] In my darkest hours, it is not the strength and power of God that I cling to, but his tenderness. Because when Jesus arrived and Mary questioned him, he didn't give her a theological treatise. He didn't chastise her for her grief. He joined her in it. And isn't that what we need when we are deep in grief? Not endless explanations, but the gentle presence of one who loves us.

Jesus' tears aren't just of grief, however. The NIV translation says that he was 'deeply moved in spirit and troubled' (v. 33), but *The Message* tells us that 'a deep anger welled up within him'. Grief and anger are not so far apart, are they? What I think we see here, as the poet Dylan Thomas puts it, is a 'raging at the dying of the light'.

Jesus is showing us that death isn't something we should get used to. It was never meant to be like this, and grief wasn't meant to fill our hearts. But sin brought with it death and all the agony that accompanies it. This is what Jesus is angry about – that love now comes at a cost. And perhaps he's thinking of the price he will pay for it in time.

In the West, we have sanitised death and grief. We don't want to accept that death is a part of our reality, as we push back at ageing and any sign that death is to come. And so we wish to compartmentalise grief too. It's allowed at funerals, for a set time and in private, lest we remind the world that death is inevitable.

It's sometimes said that Christians shouldn't grieve. But the verse this advice is taken from doesn't tell us not to grieve; it tells us to grieve differently: 'Brothers and sisters, we do not want you to be uninformed about those who sleep in death, so that you do not grieve like the rest of mankind, who have no hope' (1 Thessalonians 4:13). I would argue that as followers of Christ, the 'Man of Sorrows', Christians should be people of grief. As philosopher Nicholas Wolterstorff said in the aftermath of the death of his son: 'I shall look at the world through tears. Perhaps I shall see things that dry-eyed I could not see.'[17]

We can survey all that is far from Eden with tears in our eyes. There is a chemical difference between tears of grief and tears shed because of overzealous onion chopping. Tears of grief release something in us. We can grieve injustices and loss, but we can do so with hope.

Jesus' tears were not the end of Lazarus's story, because Jesus rolled away his tombstone and called him from death to life in a glorious miracle that points us to a world to come. A miracle where 'He will wipe every tear from their eyes. There will be no more death or mourning or crying or pain, for the old order of things has passed away' (Revelation 21:4).

There will be weeping in this world – arguably there should be weeping for all that is lost and wrong – but we need not weep and grieve without hope. May our tears of grief for all that is lost be suffused with hope because of the one who loves us enough to count each tear that falls.

Breath prayer

Inhale: Jesus wept
Exhale: He will wipe every tear

Week 15
Palm Sunday: Gentle and lowly

Reading: Luke 19:1–10

For the Son of Man came to seek and to save the lost. (v. 10)

Palm Sunday, Jesus' triumphal entry into Jerusalem, is a familiar story. There's the colt acquired for him, the cloaks lining the ground and the palms waved by people to welcome Jesus to the city – and there was no mistaking that the people were welcoming him as King. 'Hosanna!' they cried. 'Save us!' they were saying. And yet by the end of the week, they would be crying, 'Crucify him!'

It was a triumphant entry to a week that changed the world for ever, but there are clues in the manner of his entry that Jesus was to be a king like no other. As Pope Benedict XVI said: 'He is a king who destroys the weapons of war, a king of peace and a king of simplicity, a king of the poor.'[18] He's the king we need in these times, isn't he? Amid the wars and rumours of wars, the climate crisis and a mental health emergency, we are a world thirsting for the cool waters of peace.

The greatest beauty about this story for me, however, is not in the drama of the palms. It's in the few verses tucked away at the end of the passage in Luke 19:41, which tell us: 'As he approached Jerusalem and saw the city, he wept over it and said, 'If you, even you, had only known on this day what would bring you peace – but now it is hidden from your eyes.'' For Jesus' tear-filled eyes saw what those who were laying palms did not; that this journey was not going to remain celebratory. He knew that they were desperate for a warrior king to overthrow the Romans – and he knew that, instead, they were walking into a week of weeping and unimaginable pain.

At the start of what was going to be the hardest week of his time on earth, Jesus was lamenting, weeping for the people he so loved, because they didn't understand what was coming. He knew that the way of peace was going to look nothing like they expected.

It's the same for us, isn't it? We don't understand what will bring us peace even now. We so often try to numb, fight or work our way to peace, when the truth is that it can't ever be achieved by something we do. It can only come as we draw closer to the heart of Christ, who describes himself as 'gentle and lowly'.

Jesus' tears of love and lament are the cool waters of peace, and all we need to do is welcome him, trusting that the path ahead may not be the easiest, but will be the one that draws us closer to him.

Blessing

Let the righteous anger of Jesus flipping tables fuel us;
Let us be filled with the devotion of Mary's anointing.
May our cry be, 'Not my will but yours be done.'
Let us hold on to Jesus when we are tempted away.
May we stay as close to Jesus in our suffering as Mary did,
May we gather in the darkness of Holy Saturday,
May our hallelujahs rise with Jesus on resurrection day.

Week 16

Easter Sunday: Gardener God

Reading: John 20:11–18

> They asked her, 'Woman, why are you crying?'
> (v. 13)

It began in the dark.

The greatest day in history, the reason millions of people celebrate, began in the dark. It was as unexpected an entry as the Saviour of the world coming from Mary's womb. We know nothing of the moment of resurrection. We are not told how it happened or what it looked like. We only know how people discovered its wonder. This greatest miracle remains a mystery. It seems to me that this is the way God works a lot of the time. We know he can do things in spectacular fashion, but it seems he prefers the ways that will call us closer to him.

In the beginning, there was a garden, and though I'm not a gardener myself, I know gardening is slow, often imperceptible, work. Planting seeds buries them deep in the dark, covered in soil like the sealed tomb of Jesus, and the seeds break open and work their way towards the light, before finally emerging into glorious life. It's easy to miss. We look away, leave them unattended, and the next moment flowers have bloomed.

Perhaps, then, it was not just Mary Magdalene's tears that obscured her vision when she mistook the risen Lord as the gardener. Perhaps it was seeing Jesus in a role he'd always played – he was the Gardener of creation. In John's Gospel, we are told that it was the moment Jesus spoke her name that she recognised him. Yet even in that recognition, she was told not to cling to him. It would have been a situation of joy-filled confusion, with grief woven through once more as he told her he would leave again – that he would ascend to the Father.

The joy of the resurrection was not uncomplicated; it came through mistaken identities, obscured truths and the knowledge that their Lord was not going to remain with them. That's perhaps why, even after they'd heard the news of the resurrection, they remained huddled behind a locked door.

This joy, though, was not just for them. It had come to everyone. As it did then, so now it will meet us where we are in our confusion and our fear, our dashed hopes and dreams, in the dark. The coming of Jesus may not be how we expect it to be, but the work of Jesus will always be characterised by the love from which we were created in the beginning, and will be all the more beautiful because of it.

The joy of Jesus is not one of simple happiness. It's certainly not a life free of trouble. In fact, Jesus told the disciples that in this life there would be trouble! But it is a joy that comes from unshakeable hope that, even in our darkness, God is working. It's the joy that death, however dark, has been conquered by the love of God in Christ Jesus. It's the joy that tells us that because of the cross and the days in darkness, we are never to be left alone in our darkness.

The joy that comes through tears is one I can trust. It's a joy that knows what it means to hurt and knows what it means to be broken, and because of this we know it's undefeatable.

He is risen, through the darkness to life and light. He will one day raise us too. But as we wait in glorious anticipation of what is to come, we are held in the hands of the Gardener who coaxes us back to life and back to him.

Breath prayer

Inhale: He is risen
Exhale: Let our hallelujahs rise

Week 17
Second Sunday of Easter: We had hoped

Reading: Luke 24:13–25

> But we had hoped that he was the one who was going to redeem Israel. And what is more, it is the third day since all this took place.
> (v. 21)

The story of Jesus walking the road to Emmaus is one that has long captured my heart. There is something extraordinary about Jesus choosing to spend the first day of his resurrected life walking alongside two heartbroken and hopeless friends. It sets the tone for how he interacts with people post-resurrection. He meets people in their hopelessness, fear and shame to set them free – and he is still doing the same for us today.

I can imagine that Cleopas and Mary were incredulous when Jesus opened the conversation by asking them, 'What are you discussing?' (v. 17). The story of Jesus' crucifixion, and perhaps the rumours of the empty tomb, would have been inescapable in Jerusalem.

When we are urged to share in prayer with God, it is not because he does not know what we're going through. In fact, he probably knows better than we do, but his priority, as it was then, is our relationship with him. He wants us to choose to tell him the darkest and hardest paths we walk.

So Jesus chose to listen, rather than reveal himself. There is power in listening. So often, what our hurting and hopeless hearts need is someone to listen to us. Jesus listened as Cleopas said the saddest words, 'We had hoped.' They spoke of utter hopelessness and despair. Perhaps you recognise it? The diagnosis that changed your life, the relationship you lost, the pain that lingers. This kind of hopelessness can cause people to wander far from their faith; it's a splinter that causes us to pull away from God as we wrestle with the questions we can't answer. This passage shows us that amid this suffering there is comfort to be found. It's found first in the speaking of our hopelessness, and second in the presence of God, which finds us in our depths.

After listening to Cleopas's story, Jesus told his own. He walked Cleopas through everything the Scriptures said about him. I can imagine Jesus taking Cleopas through Isaiah and the passages talking about the suffering servant, recounting the words of the psalm he cried on the cross, 'My God, my God, why have you forsaken me?'[19] But even though Jesus had explained how all the Scriptures led to him, he was still not recognised. He was not recognised until he broke bread as he did on the night of his crucifixion. Although some translations say that scales fell from their eyes enabling them to recognise him, sometimes I wonder if it's because they saw his scars as he shared the bread. For we worship a God who is recognisable not just by his might, but by his willingness to enter weakness.

As with the other accounts of Jesus after his resurrection, this story is one where Jesus demonstrated what love looks like. He showed us how to love one another better in the ways he interacted with people in their darkest times.

To me, it seems that this is the message he most wanted to reaffirm; that we are his beloved and this is how we are to interact with one another if we are to call ourselves his followers. He showed us that love doesn't always look particularly pretty or elegant, but it is extravagant and willing to reach into the darkness for others.

Jesus knew that the journeys his disciples would walk wouldn't be easy and he knew that it would be their love for him and for one another that would sustain them even in death. The same is true for us today. We are to be known by how we love – in both the light and the dark times.

Blessing

Walking in their haze of grief,
All is lost.
'We had hoped.'
They had hoped he'd be their Saviour,
Yet they saw him draw his last breath.
The man who joined them listened to their hopeless cries, their pain,
Before opening his own story, joining it with theirs through the ancient Scriptures.
And yet it is not through his words that he is recognised,
But through his wounds.
His wounds that remained after the miraculous resurrection
Were the testimony that saw them recognise him.
Don't we so often recognise one another's wounds before their words?
It is the wonder of our Lord that he ministers with words and wounds,
So that we may see his power, his beauty, his kindness with our weary eyes thirsty for wonder.
May we too find our hope in his wounds as we minister with wonder.

Week 18
Third Sunday of Easter: 'Peace be with you'

Reading: John 20:19–23

> Again Jesus said, 'Peace be with you! As the Father has sent me, I am sending you.'
> (v. 21)

They were huddled together in a closed room, full of fear. They had heard rumours that Jesus was alive, but they weren't able to bring themselves to truly believe them. They couldn't understand what this meant for them and for the world around them. They hid behind closed doors, unable to move forward and perhaps unwilling to face their own actions of the past few days.

It's in passages like this one in John 20 that I can tend towards frustration with the disciples. After all they'd seen, they still struggled to believe the truth that was before them. And then I think of my own life and realise I'm no different. I too am quick to forget the glories and kindness of God I have seen when I'm confronted with a new horizon of fear. The disciples were living under the rule of fear and were unable to see that love had already set them free. Sound familiar?

The temptation to live out of our fears instead of love is great. It stalks our relationships, our work, the way we move in our bodies and the things we allow our minds to imagine. I see it most often in my parenting. My instinct is to help my little boy avoid all pain and difficulty. I want to wrap him in cotton wool so that he is kept away from harm at all costs. I want him to stay away from the high slides, to crawl along on his scooter at a snail's pace. But not only is this impractical – he is six and very sure of his own mind – to do this would not be an act of true love; it would be an act of fear. Children need small, supported risks to develop their resilience as they grow older. As psychologist Jonathan Haidt wrote in his book *The Anxious Generation*: 'Like young trees exposed to the wild, children who are routinely exposed to small risks grow up to become adults who can handle much larger risks without panicking.'[20] Loving without (or, more realistically, with less) fear means allowing those we love to take risks – even with the love we give them.

Despite all they had seen of Jesus – the miracles he'd performed and the teaching he'd given – and even though they'd heard that he had risen, the disciples huddled together and hid away. We might like to think we would have been seeking him out, asking him questions and declaring the miracle, but the likelihood is that we'd have been huddling in fear too. The trauma and perhaps guilt of the previous few days – seeing Jesus arrested, and fleeing from him in the hour of his greatest need – kept the disciples who knew him best away from him on the greatest day in history. And in his loving-kindness, Jesus' first move was not one of admonishment (although ensuring relationships are restored would come later), but one where he declared peace over them and their fear-filled hearts.

'Peace be with you,' he declared and as he did so he showed them the marks of his wounds. He was reassuring them that he was who he said he was, not through a show of strength or majesty but through his scars. Just as he did with those walking the road to Emmaus and just as he would to Thomas later on. 'Peace be with you,' he declared again and he breathed the Holy Spirit onto them.

I do not think it is a mistake that to exhale with long deep breaths calms our nervous system, as I explained earlier. It's the gear shift that moves us from fight or flight into a space where we can think more clearly. We were made for long slow breaths that allow our lungs to expand with oxygen before exhaling, until the tension in our shoulders drops. The peace of God can be felt as tangibly in our bodies as in our minds. This peace is made to be felt and shared; it's the oxygen needed to share the gospel and we need it too.

We need the Spirit of God to share the gospel of God. I don't mean that it has to be dramatic or involve a mountain-top experience of the Spirit; but we cannot share what we do not know. My own conversion, if you can call it a conversion at five years old, was in the upper room of our small Baptist church. Even at such a young age, in that moment I experienced a peace from God I can still neither articulate nor deny.

Our world so desperately needs the peace of God in these days of climate emergency, mental health crisis and countless refugees seeking their safe place. It needs peace-makers in every sphere of life, including social media platforms. I believe this is a work of love from the Spirit of God in fractious and divided times. As we go into this week, I want to end with a breath prayer, to calm minds and bodies for whatever lies ahead.

Breath prayer

Inhale: Peace
Exhale: Be with you

Inhale: Peace
Exhale: Be within you

Inhale: Peace
Exhale: Be around you

Week 19
Fourth Sunday of Easter: Jesus of the scars

Reading: John 20:24–29

> A week later his disciples were in the house again, and Thomas was with them. Though the doors were locked, Jesus came and stood among them and said, 'Peace be with you!' (v. 26)

I've always had a great fondness for Thomas. It seems to me that he's acquired a bad reputation. I can't help but think that most of us, in his situation, would have behaved in much the same way. We don't know where Thomas was when the other disciples were huddled together in fear as Jesus appeared before them, but we know he struggled to believe the others' account, and his language and disbelief sound almost indignant in our translations.

He wanted not just to see the risen Jesus, but to have proof that his resurrected body bore the marks of his death. He wanted to put his hands in the places where Jesus was pierced.

What I find remarkable is not Thomas's doubt or his desire for proof. After all, I expect if we could have our faith proven conclusively, we'd take the opportunity. I certainly would. What is remarkable is Jesus' openness to dispelling Thomas's doubts. When Jesus appeared to Thomas, it was through a closed door, so his appearance was already defying the laws of physics. We don't know whether, at that point, Jesus had heard about Thomas's words from the other disciples or he just knew, but he immediately told Thomas to touch his scars and encouraged him to see and believe.

The willingness of Jesus to show his scars has long captivated me, not least because they remained on his body post-resurrection. They are signs that he is the real deal and offer proof to Thomas, but they also tell of his journey to hell and back. It seems to me that Jesus could have emerged spotless from the tomb, but instead he carried his scars not only into his resurrection but to his place at the right hand of the Father.

Years of self-harm have left me more scarred than I care to admit, and it's taken years for me to be able to accept them as a part of the story my body carries. For many years they were a source of deep shame – even as I was travelling the country delivering self-harm awareness training. There was a disconnect between what I knew to be true (that scars were a part of my story) and what I felt in my heart about them. They were marks from the worst times of my life and I didn't want to be reminded of them. But as the years have passed, my relationship with my scars has changed. I can't say I like them, but I accept them because they are roads that I travelled to get this far.

This account of Thomas helped me to see my scars differently, because while I felt mine were signs of despair, Jesus' scars were the ultimate sign of his love for us and for the depths he was prepared to go to out of his love for us. Knowing that enabled me to see my scars differently. They are marks of the battles I've faced, but they are also a sign of God's grace, because I live to tell the tale and point to a better story in which Jesus' scars became a part of his glory. As the late Timothy Keller said:

> On the Day of the Lord – the day that God makes everything right, the day that everything sad comes untrue… you will find that the worst things that have ever happened to you will in the end only enhance your eternal delight. On that day, all of it will be turned inside out and you will know joy beyond the walls of the world. The joy of your glory will be that much greater for every scar you bear. So live in the light of the resurrection and renewal of this world, and of yourself, in a glorious, never-ending, joyful dance of grace.[21]

The risen Jesus' scars have a unique and astonishing power, not just because he had them, but because he rose with them and ascended into heaven with them. So perhaps we will have our scars in heaven – but we will only see the beauty of them.

In actual fact, Thomas doesn't seem that concerned with seeing Jesus' scars and touching his wounds. His doubt is transfigured into glorious faith as soon as he sets his eyes on Jesus. Indeed, he utters the first testimony of who the risen Jesus is: 'My Lord and my God!' (v. 28).

All throughout this exchange, Jesus doesn't chastise Thomas. He willingly offers his scars as proof, but in his final words of this account, he offers us a special word. We who believe without seeing him face to face receive a special blessing, because we trust without irrefutable proof and enter into our relationship with him in faith.

Poem

Below is an extract from a poem written in the wake of the First World War. May it guide you in your prayers this week.

> The other gods were strong; but Thou wast weak;
> They rode, but Thou didst stumble to a throne;
> But to our wounds only God's wounds can speak,
> And not a god has wounds, but Thou alone.
> ('Jesus of the Scars' by Edward Shillito, 1872–1948)[22]

Week 20
Fifth Sunday of Easter: 'Do you love me?'

Reading: John 21:15–25

> The third time he said to him, 'Simon son of John, do you love me?' Peter was hurt because Jesus asked him the third time, 'Do you love me?' He said, 'Lord, you know all things; you know that I love you.'
> (v.17)

There is a beautiful symmetry in the Gospel of John in what I imagine was rather an awkward conversation between Peter and Jesus. John 21 is often thought of as an epilogue – possibly written by someone other than John. It ties up the story's loose ends, and is a sort of 'what happened next' after the drama of Jesus' resurrection. If you remember, Peter famously denied Jesus three times after Jesus' arrest in an attempt to distance himself from the trouble.

When I think of this passage, I imagine Peter with his head down, scuffing his sandals in the sand. I can imagine him finding it hard to look Jesus in the eye knowing what he'd done. And then came the body blow: 'Simon son of John.' When he'd been called from his life as a fisherman, he was given a new name. No longer Simon, he was Peter – the Rock. Surely Jesus was reminding him here that his faith hadn't been so rock-like recently.

To add insult to injury, Jesus asked for a confirmation of Peter's love: 'Do you love me more than these?' More than these? More than these what? The other disciples? The fish that had been caught? More than the life he'd had as Simon son of John?

The commentaries tell us that the brash Peter who had declared his love loudly and enthusiastically was gone. Now Peter answered a bit more hesitantly: 'You know that I love you.' It was an affirmative answer, but it wasn't as gung-ho as the previous one. It was quieter and more considered. It can be translated as 'I'm fond of you'. It strikes me that Peter was scared to claim as much when he'd failed so dramatically. His smaller 'I love you' seems to have cost more.

I know this from my own life. When I was little I shouted to the rooftops that I loved Jesus, and I did ... but I also know how much more it cost me to say I loved God as I got older. 'I love you' was a statement of endurance as much as an utterance of praise. Bearing in mind the strength it must have taken Peter to say those words after all that had passed, you can imagine the pain he felt when Jesus asked him again: 'Do you love me?' In my mind, his response had a slight pleading note as he replied, 'Yes Lord, you *know* I love you.' And a third time: 'Simon son of John, do you love me?'

It actually says in the text that Peter was saddened by Jesus' repeated questioning. I wonder if he was remembering his third denial, followed by the sound of crowing. Jesus asked for Peter's love three times, using his old name three times. Jesus was restoring, reversing, Peter's denials and showing Peter that he was forgiven. Even though Jesus had done the impossible and risen from the dead, he still took time to forgive his friends.

He didn't just forgive us, however; he redeemed us. The word 'redeem' stems from the Latin *redimere*, which means 'to buy back'. Jesus buys back our sins, forgiving us, but more than that he gives us something in return for our failings. Peter's allegiance to the resurrected Christ was followed each time by three sheep-related sayings: 'Feed my lambs', 'Take care of my sheep' and 'Feed my sheep'. I think the shift in imagery here is very deliberate: from a fisherman to a shepherd. The image of a shepherd is used time and again throughout the Bible to describe the provision and guidance of God. Psalm 23 describes the Lord as Shepherd – the one who provides everything his flock needs, protects them from darkness and carries them home. This was the calling for Peter to take up the role of a shepherd, and pastor, in spite and perhaps in part because of all he had done. But this new season of ministry is not a happily-ever-after story. I hate to say it, but we don't get a 'happily ever after', not this side of a new creation. In the next section, Jesus informs Peter (quite brutally, I think) that things aren't going to be easy. He says that Peter will literally take up his cross to follow Christ.

If ever there was a case against knowing our future, I think it's right here in this passage. Jesus' call of 'follow me' this time seems to be referring to Peter following Jesus to death on a cross. The phrase 'stretch out your hands' was widely considered to indicate crucifixion, the death we know Peter suffered later on. Some historical sources claim that Peter was crucified upside down, feeling himself unworthy to be killed in the same manner as Jesus.

The Christian life is not an easy option. I wish it was. But there is only one answer that gives me real comfort: love. Love and suffering are inextricably linked in forgiveness and restoration. You can't have one without the other. Philosopher Nicholas Wolterstorff wrote a short book called *Lament for a Son* in the wake of his son's death. In it, he tried to reconcile the God he loved with the son he had lost and said:

> For we all prize and love; and in this present existence of ours, prizing and loving yield suffering. Love in our world is suffering love. Some do not suffer much, though, for they do not love much. Suffering is for the loving. This, said Jesus, is the command of the Holy One: 'You shall love your neighbour as yourself.' In commanding us to love, God invites us to suffer.[23]

God doesn't ask us to do what he has not already done. He is like the parent who dips their elbow into the bathwater to check the temperature. He does that for us, on a mighty and cosmic scale.

Yes, we are called to love and to suffer. But we walk in the footprints of Jesus – in the pain, in the love and, one day, in the glory. And we can experience the same saving grace that Peter did. We can live in the same spirit of boldness and faith. It's our choice and our chance to do what we can with our fresh start.

Blessing

Easter isn't over.
It's the beginning of the season of Eastertide,
Where we celebrate resurrection life.
After the stone was rolled away,
After the bread was shared,
After he had risen,
The disciples still hid in fear; Thomas still needed his scars.
We still have our doubts, our wounds, our fears.
The difference is Jesus.
Jesus in our fears, Jesus in our doubts, Jesus in our wounds.
With us always, until the very end.

Week 21
Sixth Sunday of Easter: The Great Commission

Reading: Matthew 28:16–20

'And surely I am with you always, to the very end of the age.' (v. 20)

At first glance the Great Commission can be overwhelming. It's the last conversation Jesus has with his disciples in Matthew's Gospel, when he tells them to go and make disciples and baptise them, but also says that he will never leave them. It has been the subject of countless sermons since. It's a proclamation of the work of being a Christian. It's a responsibility not to be taken lightly, but it's not one we are meant to bear alone. Bookending the Great Commission is a proclamation of who we're speaking for and an encouragement that we do it not in our power, but in the power of Jesus. In verse 18 we read: 'All authority in heaven and on earth has been given to me [Jesus].' The commission is not the words of a master commanding his people to work, but a reminder of who Jesus is and the place he holds in the heavens. The power and authority that separated the sea from the land belongs to Jesus and he speaks from this. And the passage closes with, 'And surely I am with you always, to the very end of the age.' Alongside this mission that Jesus delivered to his followers, he reminded them that he was still Emmanuel, which means 'God with us'. And even though he was leaving their sight, he was not leaving them to do this work alone. He would accompany them through it all.

We need that reassurance, don't we? Knowing that we are loved and not alone creates a boldness we cannot have without support. My friend Will van der Hart, one of the directors of the Mind and Soul Foundation, used to say regularly in his sermons that we are most dangerous for the kingdom of God when we feel most loved. Love is the power that enables us to play our part in the Great Commission. For while it was given specifically to Jesus' eleven disciples, it speaks to us all and is something we all have a role in.

Being loved gives confidence. Being secure in who we are and how we are loved enables us to take risks and be bold. As Brené Brown puts it, 'A deep sense of love and belonging is an irreducible need of all people. We are biologically, cognitively, physically, and spiritually wired to love, to be loved, and to belong. When those needs are not met, we don't function as we were meant to.'[24]

We can only fulfil our part in the Great Commission, our role in the kingdom of heaven, if we recognise and feel the power of our belovedness and Jesus' assurance that he will be with us to the very end of the age. In the middle, we have Jesus expounding what the Great Commission looks like. It's a call not just to get converts but to make disciples, baptise them and teach them to obey all that Jesus has said. It's a call to obey the law of love that can be summed up in those two commandments to love the Lord our God with all our heart, mind and strength, and to love our neighbours as ourselves. We will not all baptise people, we will not all teach people, but we can all love.

Sarah Bessey writes in her book *Field Notes for the Wilderness*: 'What would it be like to love the world not in general but in particular? Pay attention, be mindful of loving this particular world and your particular people and your particular place and your particular self. Love is not cautious but extravagant and specific.'[25] The call to love can so often feel too vast to comprehend or think about practically, so the advice to love 'in particular' is a really helpful way of framing it and I believe that Jesus sets out the particular in his teachings throughout his ministry – from the Sermon on the Mount to how he interacted with Pharisees who questioned him on the law and how he reached those most in need with his healing and his presence.

The Great Commission is not too big for us to be a part of and neither is it too vague for us to understand. It is Jesus' defining call to us and a reminder of who is calling us. Jesus is the one who was there in the beginning, and he is the one who will be with us until the end. And he asks us to be a part of his work of love for the whole world.

Breath prayer

Inhale: In your authority
Exhale: Let me love in the particular

Week 22
Ascension Sunday: Jesus' coronation

Reading: Luke 24:36–53

> While he was blessing them, he left them and was taken up into heaven.
> (v. 51)

The ascension is one of those points in the Christian calendar that often gets overlooked. It somehow goes under the radar for many of us and only occupies a few verses of Scripture, but it is another pivotal moment in the story of God. Author and pastor Glenn Packiam says that perhaps we don't connect to the ascension like we do to Christmas or Pentecost because it's a story of Jesus leaving. All the other festivals celebrate God's arrival (Jesus' coming at Christmas, Jesus' return from the grave at Easter and the Holy Spirit's coming at Pentecost). Packiam points out that 'the ascension of Jesus can feel like Jesus is escaping earth and abandoning us'.[26]

We crave the nearness of Jesus. At least I do. The stories of him stooping to earth as a baby, of him weeping and coming close to the hurting and the least of us, reach my heart in a way that I think I miss about the ascension. I expect that I would have been like Mary Magdalene at the empty tomb, tempted to hold on to Jesus even when he told her not to.

But I admit that in neglecting the ascension I've missed an important part of Jesus' story. We need his life, his death, his resurrection and his ascension because it's the completion of his earthly mission by returning to the right hand of the Father and preparing a place for us.

The ascension is Jesus' coronation. It tells us that Jesus was (and is) not just fully and perfectly human, but fully and perfectly our King of kings.

The coronation of King Charles in 2023 was a spectacle to behold, but it was also mysterious to us. There was so much history we could not fully grasp; each action was heavy with meaning. The ascension of Jesus is a bit like that: heavy with meaning we can't completely comprehend, but glorious partly because of its mystery. As R. C. Sproul said:

> The climax of Jesus' earthly ministry came when He ascended to heaven and sat down at the right hand of God. This was His investiture, His coronation, when the Father crowned Him as King of kings and Lord of lords. It was at that moment that Jesus' glory was restored to Him in His heavenly kingdom.[27]

If you've not seen the film *The Lion King*, I recommend it. The young Simba becomes king as soon as his father, Mufasa, dies. He is king even as he wanders into the wilderness and befriends Timon and Pumbaa. But Simba doesn't install himself as king until right at the end of the film when he ascends Pride Rock. He's been king all along, but he isn't crowned until the point in the film that brings it full circle. The same is true for Jesus. He'd been King all along, but the ascension was his crowning.

Ascension brings together realities of Jesus that are so hard for us to reconcile. He is meekness and majesty, manhood and deity. It is what makes the God of the Bible distinct from the gods of any other religion, or those we make ourselves. He has experienced every breath of humanity, but is now ascended to the very heights of all that is heavenly, and in doing so he takes what it means to be human to the very heart of God.

It's confusing and hard to comprehend, yes; but it is a reminder of the breadth and depth of the God we worship, who knows us intimately but who is himself unknowable. Jesus has retaken his rightful place on the throne and in seeming to draw away from his earthly disciples, he draws closer to the whole of humanity.

Prayer

He ascended
But he did not abandon.
Even in his leaving
He promised a new presence.
He returned to glory,
But his unending kindness,
His unquenchable hope,
His unfathomable love
Remains with us.

Week 23
Pentecost: Glimpse of the kingdom

Reading: Acts 2:1–13

> All of them were filled with the Holy Spirit and began to speak in other tongues as the Spirit enabled them.
> (v. 4)

Pentecost is often known as the birthday of the Church. It's a day of celebration and joy, when we come together to remember the Spirit coming in glorious power. Pentecost ushers in a new era for the people of God and opens the arms of the family of God – no longer to be channelled through a single people group but blowing through the world and available to everyone. In some ways it's a surprising move, a drastic change of direction compared with how God revealed himself through Jesus. And yet the extravagance of Pentecost is fully in keeping with the extravagant love seen in Jesus' teachings when he spoke of abandoning the ninety-nine to reach the one lost.

In the coming of this new age, however, we are reminded that the Holy Spirit is not someone new – he's been there all along. The way the Spirit comes at Pentecost is meant to make us zoom out and see that he was always there. In the same way that the Spirit set the bush ablaze before Moses, the wind and fire on Mount Sinai and the column of fire that appeared when the Temple was built, this was a dramatic show of God's power. When there appeared to be tongues of fire at Pentecost, it was showing that this was not a new God – it was Yahweh.

It's not only the wind and fire that connect Pentecost to the bigger story of God moving. Verse 4 tells us, 'All of them were filled with the Holy Spirit and began to speak in other tongues as the Spirit enabled them.' It's this detail that has always captivated me. So much so, I wrote a whole essay on it back in my Bible college days. As the Spirit fell and the people in the crowd began to speak to one another in countless different languages, I believe this was meant to represent God bringing his Church together in unity as a reversal of the scattering of people at Babel.

In Genesis 11 we read that until that point the whole world spoke in a single language, but they used this commonality to try to reach God. Verse 4 says: 'Come, let us build ourselves a city, with a tower that reaches to the heavens, so that we may make a name for ourselves; otherwise we will be scattered over the face of the whole earth.' This desire to make a name for themselves, to come together and reach the heavens, wasn't with a view to honouring God. It was to elevate their status and proximity to power. The result was that God muddled their languages and the people scattered across the globe, never again able to come together easily in a common language.

At Babel, the people tried to reach the heavens, but at Pentecost, God's Spirit fell upon the people. At Babel, the people used the common language to raise themselves up and make their own name and national identity, but at Pentecost God poured his Spirit down so that people of different nations and languages could communicate the glory of God to the whole world.

Pentecost is a glorious glimpse of what the kingdom of God will look like and what our churches can show to the world. God did not reverse Babel by giving a new common language. He did it by showing understanding of each language present. God's love doesn't make us homogeneous; it makes us diverse and united.

Pentecost does what the best birthday celebrations do: it looks back at what has come before and forward to what is possible. The Spirit of God is not a new deity, but a part of the Trinity, Father, Son and Spirit, that we worship as one, and which will one day return in glory, bringing the kingdom of God to earth to reign for evermore.

A blessing for Pentecost

This power came like the wind,
Like the breath that first enlivened us.
This power came with the promise
Of inescapable presence.
This power comes like fire
To warm and energise.
This power comes with the hope
Of healing what divides.
This power comes as helper and counsellor
With gentleness and goodness.
This power comes to be shared
With love everlasting,
Peace all-encompassing,
Joy irrepressible.

Week 24
Trinity Sunday: Eternal life

Reading: John 3:1–21

> He came to Jesus at night and said, 'Rabbi, we know that you are a teacher who has come from God. For no one could perform the signs you are doing if God were not with him.' (v. 2)

We don't know why Nicodemus came to Jesus under the cover of night, but as a Pharisee and a teacher, we do know that he would have been pretty confident in his beliefs. But he also seemed to be deeply curious about the claims Jesus was making. Was there some shame in a member of the Jewish leadership having questions about the faith he was seen to be an expert in? It can feel awkward to ask questions, can't it? Especially when we feel that we should know it all already, or at the very least know more than we do. For those of us who have been Christians for a long time, we can sometimes feel less able to ask questions rather than finding it easier.

Jesus' teaching on being born again and being born in the Spirit initially provoked confusion in Nicodemus. 'How can this be?' he asks in John 3:9. But Jesus reminded Nicodemus that in the same way he didn't do anything to be born physically, it wasn't his work or his goodness that was going to help him be born again. Nicodemus wasn't expecting to be told that he needed to do anything more than he already was – he followed the law, so he thought he was doing everything right. But doing 'the right thing' and knowing 'the right stuff' isn't the way into the kingdom of God. The only way is to be saved through Jesus. Everyone needs Jesus equally: lawyers and vicars, criminals and business people, me and you.

This truth didn't look the way Nicodemus expected it to, and it didn't sound the way he'd always been taught. And yet it was the offer of more freedom than he could ever have imagined. The words Jesus said next are some of the most quoted from Scripture, but they remain so hard to grasp: 'For God so loved the world that he gave his one and only Son, that whoever believes in him shall not perish but have eternal life' (John 3:16). All of it – being born again, having eternal life – is for no other reason than we are loved by God. Love is the reason God sent his Son. Love is the reason that God wants us to join him in eternity. We were created for this.

It's hard to get our heads and hearts around the fact that we were made for a great love we can never fully comprehend. From the Father, through the Son and by the Spirit. Even a sliver of understanding about this love cannot help but change everything, and it did for Nicodemus.

Later in John 7 we read of him defending Jesus, but even more importantly he accompanied Joseph of Arimathea to wrap Jesus' body with spices and linen after his crucifixion. His life was changed by his understanding of how God loved the world and him. Will we allow our lives to be changed by God's love?

Blessing

Sometimes the gospel doesn't feel like good news.
Sometimes the healing doesn't look like a cure.
Sometimes the gospel comes like John's voice in the desert:
Uncomfortable truths and wild.
At others it comes like the waiting and the hoping of all the years
For 'God with us'.
Sometimes healing comes with a sting,
Sometimes like a soothing balm,
And yet however it comes, the gospel is good, because we can trust that it comes.
It is love from the Father, through the Son, by the Holy Spirit.

Week 25
Ordinary Time: Love

Reading: 1 Corinthians 13

> And now these three remain: faith, hope and love. But the greatest of these is love.
> (v. 13)

Over the coming weeks, we're going to explore the facets of love described in possibly the most famous passage about love:

> Love is patient, love is kind. It does not envy, it does not boast, it is not proud. It does not dishonour others, it is not self-seeking, it is not easily angered, it keeps no record of wrongs. Love does not delight in evil but rejoices with the truth. It always protects, always trusts, always hopes, always perseveres. Love never fails.
> (1 Corinthians 13:4–8)

It's one of those passages that is recited and quoted so often it can be tempting to think we understand it better than we do. Still, the love described in these verses is far from wishy-washy. It's a powerful manifesto of how we are meant to demonstrate our belovedness through loving others. It's a reminder that being beloved by God, while not contingent on anything we do, can and should inspire us to love ourselves and others more fully.

In the verse immediately before the chapter begins, we read: 'And yet I will show you the most excellent way.' The way of love is the excellent way, the only way to live well, and these verses show us what that looks like practically.

It's a reminder that love is inherently practical; 'to love' is a verb and it requires commitment and practice to put it into action. We can feel love easily at times: when life is going well, when we're in love with our partner, when our children are behaving or when our friends and family are easy to be with. It can feel as if love doesn't require discipline or attention during these times. But when the going gets tough, or time wears away romance and enchantment, loving can be more difficult and need more attention.

My husband and I have recently pondered the reason for the so-called 'seven-year itch' in romantic relationships. We passed that point some time ago, but were wondering if that's the magic amount of time it takes for 'cute' things to become annoying and all your wedding gifts to start breaking! But in all seriousness, love in any form often requires more from us than we have. During the coronavirus lockdowns, loving my friends and my child took me firmly outside of convenience, meaning that we spent far too much time at the opposite ends of playgrounds in the pouring rain just to have a shouted conversation!

The most excellent way of loving, as described by Paul, is demanding. Even just one of the attributes is demanding, especially patience if you're anything like me! But the truth of love is that we are only able to do it because God first loved us. As we read in 1 John 4:10–11: 'This is love: not that we loved God, but that he loved us and sent his Son as an atoning sacrifice for our sins. Dear friends, since God so loved us, we also ought to love one another.' It's good news for us that our love for others doesn't rely on our reserves of patience, perseverance or kindness, but instead on the love of God.

The love of God is the source of all the love in the world – between friends, boyfriends and girlfriends, parents and children, neighbours, and colleagues. God did not just leave us to figure out for ourselves what love looks like. He first gave the law to direct our hearts and actions in love and then, supremely, sent Jesus, who showed us what perfect love looks like in the flesh.

Prayer

God of loving-kindness,
Meet us
As the shore welcomes the waves.

Week 26

Ordinary Time: Love is patient

Reading: Romans 8:18–25

> I consider that our present sufferings are not worth comparing with the glory that will be revealed in us.
> (v. 18)

Of all the attributes of love Paul describes in his letter to the Corinthians, I'd argue that patience is the one that most of us struggle with. In fact, our whole world seems to struggle with patience. We are less inclined to wait now than we were a decade ago, as next-day delivery, Deliveroo and drive-through Starbucks have enabled and encouraged speed and efficiency instead of waiting in line. We've become poorer in time and richer in efficiency. While on holiday once with my son, he announced: 'I hate the countryside – it has no internet!' In response, I found myself explaining that when I was growing up there was no such thing as next-day delivery. I felt both old and somewhat nostalgic for a time when everything wasn't available at the touch of a button.

For most of us, patience is required in both the trivial and the significant times of our lives. Perhaps the times we are stuck in traffic, the queues, are a way of stretching the muscles of our patience to prepare us for when we need to employ it for life-changing results. We all experience seasons of struggle that push us to the limits of our endurance.

I trust these words from Paul, because he understood what it meant to be patient under the most testing of circumstances. He was not being glib when he said that 'our present sufferings are not worth comparing with the glory that will be revealed in us'.

He had experienced wrongful imprisonment and persecution, and still believed that waiting with patience for the glory that he hoped for was worth it. He understood that hope and patience were intimately connected. We cannot have one without the other.

To wait patiently, we have to believe in the hope that change will come. Perhaps that was the Israelites' problem as they travelled the long road through the wilderness. Maybe they lost hope that they would ever see the Promised Land. They bemoaned the manna that sustained them because they began to believe that it was all they would ever eat.

Aren't we the same? We grow weary of the patience required to endure in the way Paul describes. Instead we begin to believe that nothing will improve and there's nothing worth being patient for. I see it in my little boy, even though he has memories of his dad and me keeping our promises to him – like when we've told him that a park trip is coming, but he loses sight of it and despairs. He often employs a characteristic dramatic flair that I fear he's inherited from me. Present trouble, whether it be a loss in the belief that your parents will ever take you to the park, or the pain of waiting for treatment to take effect or relationships to heal, often obscures the truth of God's promises. It can make patience all the more difficult to practise and hope feel harder to hold on to.

However, Paul makes it clear what enables our hope. The pain of patience is not one of death and destruction – although it may feel similar. It is productive pain likened to that of childbirth. This doesn't lessen the pain, but it makes hope possible, because there is the promise of new life rather than the decay that leads to death.

When I was in the midst of labour pains with my son (which, contrary to popular wisdom, I have not forgotten), the promise and hope of the baby helped me to endure the long and difficult labour. Don't get me wrong, after two days with no sign of a baby, I still needed an epidural, but what powered my patience was the hope of holding my son at long last. The hope of life enabled my patience through the pain that felt like death, and this is what Paul promises of the patience of God's love and the love we can offer one another – it leads us to life.

Blessing

Blessed are you, tired of waiting,
Those hoping against hope;
For the weary ones,
For the wandering ones.

Blessed are you.
May your weariness be enlivened by wonder,
May your soul be welcomed to peace
By the one who calmed the waves.
May you find your home in him.

Week 27
Ordinary Time: Love is kind

Reading: Ruth 1

> But Ruth replied, 'Don't urge me to leave you or to turn back from you. Where you go I will go, and where you stay I will stay. Your people will be my people and your God my God.' (v. 16)

In my opinion, kindness is a severely underrated virtue. All too often, it's seen as something soft and fluffy, even weak. And yet the kindness that is described in the Bible is *khesed*, meaning 'loving-kindness' and 'loyalty'. We read of it 245 times in the Old Testament and most of the time it refers to how God loves us, but it also includes how we can love one another when it is an expression of our character. It's not something we can just do once; it flows from who we are.

One of the most beautiful examples for me of *khesed* is found in the book of Ruth. We see it in Naomi's treatment of her sons' wives when, in a short period of time, Naomi was widowed and both of her sons died. She advised her daughters-in-law, Ruth and Orpah, to return to their homeland so that they could have the chance of meeting new husbands which, in their society, would give them a security and position they could not achieve alone.

She prayed, 'May the Lord show you kindness,' giving the blessing of Israel's Lord to them both. (v. 8)

Perhaps the most famous kindness shown in the book is when Ruth remained with her mother-in-law Naomi and accompanied her back to Canaan. It was a selfless act, leaving her homeland for an unfamiliar place, to stay with her mother-in-law as they both grieved, so that she would not be alone. It was an extraordinary kindness. There is no hint of condemnation for Orpah, who did return to her homeland. What Ruth did was unexpected and full of mercy.

One of the kindest things we can do for those who are grieving is to offer our presence in the deep loneliness of loss. Naomi's loss was profound. So much so that she asked to be called Mara, which means 'bitter', to reflect that she was returning to her homeland a changed and damaged woman. But curiously, the name also means 'strength', so she returned home grieving and bitter but with an acknowledgement that she was stronger for the loss and pain she had endured.

It is often an uncomfortable realisation that our most damaging losses can also cultivate greater strength. It's not something that happens automatically. We cannot develop strength amid adversity without the presence of loving-kindness from those around us, both humanly speaking and from the Lord who embodies this kindness. Kindness is inextricable from love, because love itself is kindness and vice versa. The kindness we receive from God and those around us is a sign of their love for us and can be a sign of our love for them if we enact it.

In the times when I've been most unwell, I've received immeasurable kindness from those who love me and those who love God. There have been meals and lifts provided, toys and play dates for my little boy, and respite for my husband. These things may seem small, but have made more difference than we could describe. Loving-kindness isn't just found in the big things, like moving to another country with your widowed mother-in-law. It's found in a million tiny actions that people do all over the world: picking up a friend's favourite coffee, babysitting for new parents, sending a funny meme, helping people move house or making time to listen to someone who is hurting. It's a gift we can all receive, but also one we can all give from our own belovedness.

Breath prayer

(inspired by Psalm 36)

Inhale: Your kindness
Exhale: Extends to the skies

Week 28
Ordinary Time: Love does not boast

Reading: Galatians 6:11–18

> May I never boast except in the cross of our Lord Jesus Christ, through which the world has been crucified to me, and I to the world.
> (v. 14)

I've probably been most aware of the human tendency towards boasting (including my own) at baby groups. Picture the scene: you're sleep-deprived, bewildered and running on caffeine and baby smiles. The saying 'the days are long but the years are short' rings in your head as you try desperately to cherish every moment … even when those moments consist of filling precious minutes when your baby is asleep with attempting to tidy your house, which somehow resembles the Early Learning Centre.

Baby groups are places of refuge. They're where you can have adult conversations, even if most of those 'adult' conversations are about sleep schedules and toileting. They provide you with a hot drink and allow you to exhale in the knowledge that you're not alone in Googling 'When is the right age for a baby to sit/stand/crawl/walk?' incessantly.

During the first year of my son's life, these groups were the highlight of my week, and yet I began to recognise something in myself that I'm not sure I'd been aware of before. It was a subtle competitiveness, a desire for one-upmanship that slipped through my defences. I wanted to prove myself as a parent and I found myself engaging in endless conversations where I wanted to show off the milestones my son was hitting. If a fellow mum talked about how her baby was already crawling, I found myself rushing in with a story about how my son was trying to stand.

And while on one level I think most parents find themselves boasting about their children, there was something about this inner competitiveness that concerned me. I wanted my son to be seen for more than he was, when in reality he was (and is) more than enough. He certainly didn't need my boasts. They weren't for his benefit. They were to assuage my own feelings – feelings I expect are shared by many – that I wasn't doing enough as a mum.

Boasting is one of those parts of 'what love isn't' that slip under the radar. It doesn't seem to do a great deal of damage, so we can be tempted to ignore it. And yet I think there's a reason it's included in this list of things that love is not. Boasting is often rooted in our insecurity and seeks to find that security in being better than others, rather than in being content with our own gifts, circumstances and belovedness.

In the Bible, we see a fair amount of boasting. It's always responded to in the same way – that the only thing we can boast about is the Lord. We see God telling Gideon he has too many fighters, or Paul warning the Corinthians not to boast in him or Apollos. They should boast only in God and his love. Boasting in the power of God is done out of love and a desire to build community. Boasting in ourselves (or our children) can only ever lead to dragging others down and damaging community.

Love doesn't include us boasting about ourselves, because it pulls people apart and further away from love, whereas boasting about God, and telling the story of God's greatness, draws people towards the love that is found in Jesus. Paul makes this point to the Galatians as he seeks to keep them united in the face of arguments about how Gentiles (non-Jews) can become followers of Jesus. Galatians 6:14 proclaims, 'May I never boast except in the cross of our Lord Jesus Christ, through which the world has been crucified to me, and I to the world.'

For those interested, my son did learn to crawl and walk and do all the usual things, but we have learned that he tends to like to do them in his own sweet time. It's another reminder that boasting about achievements (his or mine) does nothing to hasten progress. It simply tends to take the joy out of the moment we're living in.

Prayer

Consider using verses from Jeremiah as your prayer today:

> 'Let not the wise boast of their wisdom
> or the strong boast of their strength
> or the rich boast of their riches,
> but let the one who boasts boast about this:
> that they have the understanding to know me,
> that I am the LORD, who exercises kindness,
> justice and righteousness on earth,
> for in these I delight,'
> declares the LORD.
> (Jeremiah 9:23–24)

Week 29
Ordinary Time: Love is not proud

Reading: 1 Peter 5:5–7

> Humble yourselves, therefore, under God's mighty hand, that he may lift you up in due time.
> (v. 6)

I have a funny relationship with pride. I am prone to thinking it's not really a problem for me. I don't often think highly of myself – sometimes quite the opposite. I don't spend time telling everyone how great I am or staring at my reflection in the mirror. But I'm beginning to learn that pride is more than thinking about yourself too highly. Too often we miss the fact that pride also looks like believing we can do it all and be it all; that we can take the place of God and somehow know better than him. That's definitely something I'm guilty of. I'm all too aware of my predisposition towards self-sufficiency and thinking that I know best. My pride doesn't necessarily result in me thinking I'm the best, but I might think I know best or know something about myself that even God himself cannot.

Thankfully, in my more objective thinking, I can see that this doesn't quite stack up. I (shocker) don't know better than God, the Creator of the universe! But it's endlessly tempting to believe that we don't need anyone; that we can fix ourselves and the problems of the world without the one who crafted everything.

We see examples of this throughout the Bible – from the Israelites' belief that it was better to worship their golden calf than wait for God's law from Moses to Peter's insistence that he would never betray Jesus. Humanity tends to think it can do without God. All too often we only recognise and realise our pride in hindsight. I look back and see how my stubborn decisions to do things my way have just caused more pain and frustration. I keep working without taking a Sabbath, because I believe the myth that I'm superhuman. Or I decide that I can power through pain alone without accepting the help that is offered so I don't appear weak or needy. Unfortunately, I'm also a slow learner, so I keep making the same mistakes. I wonder whether you find yourself in the same position?

In 1 Peter 5:5b we're told, 'Clothe yourselves, all of you, with humility toward one another, for "God opposes the proud but gives grace to the humble"' (ESV). This verse tells us that the very thing we need the most when we're struggling is his grace, and it comes to us when we are humble enough to admit our need for it. This isn't the gospel of God helping those who help themselves. It's the gospel of the God who stands at the door and knocks; who waits to be asked even though he knows that his plans are the best ones. This is the character of the God who asks us to trust him; who doesn't barge in uninvited but waits until we fall into his arms, taking the weight of our anxieties because he cares.

Our pride rejects the care of the Shepherd who leads us beside still waters and accompanies us through the dark valleys, because we think we ought to be able to do it alone or because we think there is some honour in not bothering God with our anxieties.

As I write, I'm recalling that when I was a small girl, I refused to pray for myself because I thought that God needed to focus on the Rwandan genocide. While I thought I was being noble, all I was doing was believing that I was less in need of God. It's not something I've got much better at as I've grown older, but I have become more aware of it; more aware of my need and my lack – and in tandem more amazed at God's wisdom and provision.

As the community of God, we need to remember that none of us can do this journey of life alone. We simply weren't designed that way. While holding on to our pride can do nothing but isolate us, letting go of it means that we are able to live our lives connected and reliant on God and one another.

Prayer

Creator God,
you made us all in your image:
may we discern you in all that we see,
and serve you in all that we do;
through Jesus Christ our Lord.
Amen.[28]

Week 30
Ordinary Time: Love does not dishonour

Reading: Proverbs 3:1–12

> Trust in the LORD with all your heart and lean not on your own understanding;
> in all your ways submit to him, and he will make your paths straight.
> (vv. 5–6)

The idea of honour and dishonour can feel a little alien in our contemporary culture. I can be tempted to think of it as a relic of the past or something wrapped up with our reputation. But that's not the whole picture. When Paul wrote that love does not dishonour, it isn't about external image management. It's not dragging others down so that we can be elevated, or heaping shame on people who desperately need grace (that is to say, all of us). It's about refraining from doing things in God's name that are contrary to his character.

Many of the references in Scripture about dishonour concern how and when to have sex – or rather when not to have sex. Leviticus talks quite a lot about not having sex with members of your own family, which I think we can all agree on.

But behind these laws and instructions is the desire for God's people to love one another in a way that shows the kind of love we receive from God. It's faithfully representing the love of God in the best way we can, showing it for the holy and beautiful love it is. When we fail to love in a way that honours God, we fail to love, because God is love.

So how do we honour God? We make the decision. It's as easy and as difficult as that. Proverbs 3:5 instructs us: 'Trust in the LORD with all your heart and lean not on your own understanding.' Honouring God begins with trusting God as the Lord over heaven and earth. It is perhaps the hardest thing of all, because in trusting God we relinquish control over our own lives.

I don't know about you, but I'm not a fan of relinquishing control. I like to know what's happening, when and how. But over the past few years I have become all too accustomed to the feeling of being completely out of control.

First, I had a baby. Anyone who's had one or been near one will know how that strips away most of your power. You cannot force a newborn to sleep, eat, poop – or do anything really! You just have to lean into their rhythms and somehow find your way. You still have no control, but it gets, if not easier, easier to bear.

Second, we experienced the Covid-19 pandemic. It stripped power from us in ways we would never have believed possible. During the worst of it, there was an image going around that said something like: 'We're all in the same storm, but we're not in the same ship.' We all faced restrictions, but some did it from the comfort of spacious homes and gardens, while others did so in cramped apartments with no outside space of their own.

And third, I live with chronic illness that likes to pull the rug from beneath me at the most inopportune times. This is perhaps what made me consign to the bin my idea that we have control, because none of us do. Sure, we have the illusion of control much of the time, but none of us are protected from freak accidents, illnesses or various other hardships that can befall us.

In the face of our lack of control, the idea of trusting God feels less like risk and more like comfort. Honouring God with our trust is less of a burden and more of a blessing, even when it doesn't feel that way. We're not trusting ourselves to someone without a track record, but to the one who created us. When something breaks, be it our boiler or our computer, the best people to call on for repair are often those who had a hand in creating them. They know the intricacies like no one else. In loving God and choosing to honour him with our love and trust, we're putting ourselves back in the hands of our Creator. We are trusting that he knows what is best for us because he made us. It doesn't necessarily make the choice any easier, but it allows us to relinquish control. I am able to do this because I know that ultimately God knows me better than I know myself and he knows what's best for me better than I do. I try (though I often fail) not to dishonour God with my distrust, because I begin with the knowledge that he loves me and wants what's best for me – and for you too.

Prayer

Lord, help us
To honour you
In our waking,
In our working.

Lord, help us
To submit
Our world
To your will,
To your word.

Week 31
Ordinary Time: Love is not self-seeking

Reading: Philippians 2:1–11

> Who, being in very nature God, did not consider equality with God something to be used to his own advantage.
> (v. 6)

If you attend a church even semi-regularly, it's likely you've heard a sermon or two on the topic of unity. We all know that unity lies at the heart of true community. This doesn't mean we all think the same, but it does mean we are able to come together and recognise our differences and work towards a common goal.

It's something the earliest churches recognised pretty quickly: to make any difference in the world and for God, they had to be united in mission and character. This is also something anyone who looks after a child will tell you. If the grown-ups in the room are saying different things, the child will most likely ignore them all. But if you can get on the same page, there is a chance (and let's face it, it is still just a chance) your small people will listen and get on board with what you're trying to do.

The only way we can get to any kind of unity is through selflessness, because if the aim is promoting ourselves and our own ideals, we are likely (metaphorically or literally) to push aside those with any difference of opinion. In his letter to the Philippians, Paul spends a fair amount of time encouraging unity and, by extension, humility. Because unity is impossible without humility.

I used to have some dodgy and distinctly unhelpful views about humility. I thought that in order to be 'a good Christian' I had to not only think of myself less, but think of myself badly. I believed that acknowledging any goodness in me was self-seeking and the opposite to the humility I knew was so valued in the kingdom of God. It worked well for me, because it told the same story my own mental illness was speaking over me: that I wasn't good enough. I believed that by recognising there was nothing good in me I was doing what God wanted me to do.

But as the saying goes: 'Humility is not thinking less of yourself; it is thinking of yourself less. Humility is thinking more of others.'[29] This description of humility is far more in line with what Paul was trying to tell the Philippians. They were filled with their own sense of importance instead of the servant-heartedness of Christ. It doesn't mean we don't think of ourselves at all, but we think of ourselves in proportion.

Verses 6–11 are a hymn that praises and demonstrates the kind of humility Jesus showed. It wasn't full of self-loathing, but instead it loved in a way that put the whole world first. It's interesting to me that this didn't mean Jesus neglected himself. We read countless times about Jesus withdrawing to pray. But Jesus loved those around him, before him and beyond him in a way that recognised the inherent value and worth of every human being, because each one is created in the image of God. It is only with humility, with valuing ourselves and others as precious creations rather than commodities, that we can have unity.

Unity demands that we come together in a way that respects the other's place and importance. There is a somewhat tongue-in-cheek Charlie Brown sketch that speaks about the lack of strength of five individual fingers transforming into something considerably stronger when they unite into a fist. They are described as becoming 'a weapon that is terrible to behold'. Churches where members and leaders fight one another for importance, prominence and platform cannot love in the way Jesus calls us to, because each part seeks to put itself first, front and centre. In contrast, when we all bend like the fingers of a fist we come closer to one another.

When we pull together, we love one another better, because the love that Paul describes does draw us closer than is comfortable. It allows us, on bended knee, to draw closer to the King of kings too.

Prayer

God is good
All the time.
All the time
God is good.
'You have searched me, LORD,
and you know me.
You know when I sit down and when I rise;
you perceive my thoughts from afar.
You discern my going out and my lying down;
you are familiar with all my ways.'
(Psalm 139:1–3)

Week 32
Ordinary Time: Love is not easily angered

Reading: Ephesians 4:17–32

> 'In your anger do not sin': do not let the sun go down while you are still angry.
> (v. 26)

From a quick glance at Scripture, it's all too easy to conclude that anger is the antithesis of God's love. You might even have heard teaching prohibiting anger. But the truth is a little more nuanced.

We were created to experience the whole spectrum of human emotion, from the sweetest joy to the deepest grief and rawest anger. Ephesians 4:26, quoted above, is often used to claim that all anger is sinful. But this verse is not a denial of anger or a demand never to feel angry; it is advice on how to manage anger well and without sin. Paul was writing from prison, to a church he knew well, to confront the issues they were facing with the gifts God had bestowed upon them.

The philosopher Aristotle described the conditions (and the difficulty) of not sinning while you're angry: 'Anyone can become angry … That is easy. But to be angry with the right person, to the right degree, at the right time, for the right purpose, and in the right way – that is not easy.'[30] It's not that anger in and of itself is sinful but how anger can fuel sin. Being angry at the level of poverty in the world, or at violence against women and girls, can inspire change in legislation or attitudes when it is directed appropriately. Ideally it wouldn't be powered by a desire for revenge. But as Aristotle pointed out, getting the balance right in a way that isn't malevolent is hard work.

The love Paul is talking about here is a love that isn't easily irritated and doesn't cause people to fly off the handle or hold a grudge. It isn't the anger that's sinful but the actions the anger can cause. We need anger to see a change in the world. Arguably I would not have founded the mental health awareness charity that I ran for a decade if it weren't for the anger I felt at the very obvious imbalance in how mental and physical illnesses are treated. But in the same breath, that anger had to be controlled and managed in order to effect any real change. Ranting sometimes helped get the feelings off my chest, but what made a real difference was the slow and calm work in changing attitudes in churches by being faithful to Scripture. I wonder if the same is true for you. Is there something you're passionate about that makes you angry but needs channelling to effect real and lasting change?

As I write, I can't help but think of how true this is in my parenting. Disciplining and teaching my little boy is done most effectively when I respond at the right time and in a way that he understands. It doesn't help if I shout just because he's made me cross – although if I'm honest, there is still some of that too! Love isn't easily angered, it's not trivially annoyed, but it does respond to injustice and wrongdoing. Learning the difference is a key part of loving well.

It's also how we are loved by God. God has emotions, but he isn't controlled by them. His opinion isn't swayed by his passing feelings. He is angered by injustice, but it doesn't make him withhold his mercy from those who love him. This is the God we serve and the God we are loved by. He is moved by injustice, but does not turn his back on mercy due to anger. As the author Michael Card says: 'Nowhere in scripture does it say God does not get angry. But that anger does not characterise who he is.'[31] This is the God we are loved by. He can be trusted unreservedly to act out of love and not passing anger.

Blessing

May we know the peace of the Spirit
Which calms our rising tempers.
May we know the love of the Father
Which holds all of our emotions.
May we know the hope of the Son
Which travels through our lives.

Week 33
Ordinary Time: Love does not delight in evil

Reading: Jonah 4:1–11

> I knew that you are a gracious and compassionate God, slow to anger and abounding in love, a God who relents from sending calamity.
> (v. 2b)

'Schadenfreude' is the wonderful-sounding German word that means 'delighting in evil'. It is to gain pleasure from someone's pain, and a literal translation combines *Schaden*, which means 'damage', and *Freude*, which means 'joy'.[32] Delighting in evil is to quite literally derive joy from someone's damage.

We might feel this way when we see the person we dislike voted off our favourite reality show or we secretly relish someone getting their comeuppance in a drama. This kind of delight, however, is not found in achieving justice but in that secret feeling of 'I'm glad it wasn't me!' It's the way we feel as the car in front of us is flashed by the speed camera but we escape it.

Proverbs 24:17–18 is clear when it warns the reader: 'Do not gloat when your enemy falls; when they stumble, do not let your heart rejoice, or the Lord will see and disapprove and turn his wrath away from them.' It's posited that this proverb is about David not rejoicing in the death of King Saul – even though Saul had been on a mission to murder him. David wasn't glad when Saul was killed; he participated in the mourning rituals for his king and the father of his friend Jonathan by tearing his clothes, weeping and fasting.

David didn't delight in the evil of Saul's death, because he was well aware that he too was subject to the judgement of God, which is inseparable from the love of God. And while we may not be rejoicing in such dramatic events, we can all be guilty of feeling a thrill of excitement when someone runs into bad lack or consequence. For example, celebrity magazines – a guilty waiting-room pleasure of mine – are a form of Schadenfreude. The news of break-ups, fashion faux-pas and lost jobs is seen as entertainment. It's easy to gloat when those who seem to have it all demonstrate they aren't perfect. It can almost be comforting to know that they face problems similar to ours.

But rejoicing in someone else's troubles (however trivial) isn't loving. It doesn't view those around us as humans created by God with inherent value and dignity. Delighting in evil can sound like something dramatic and uncommon, but in reality it's an everyday occurrence. We even see it in Scripture, when Jonah was ready to watch the destruction of Nineveh, which he felt it deserved. You might be familiar with the story of Jonah being swallowed by a large fish when he attempted to flee the mission God had given him to offer mercy to the Ninevite people. After exiting the fish he did go on to complete the mission God had given to him, but he wasn't pleased about it. Jonah wanted to see the punishment of the Ninevites – not the mercy that was offered.

Perhaps one of the most difficult aspects of Jonah's story is the lack of resolution. We don't read that Jonah eventually found peace amid his dissatisfaction with God's mercy. His last words are, 'And I'm so angry I wish I were dead' (Jonah 4:9). It seems he was still desperate for the Ninevites to get their just deserts.

Despite this, there is no sign of God withdrawing his mercy from the Ninevites, and Jonah did not get to see them receive the punishment he felt was warranted. What the text doesn't tell us is if Jonah ever came to terms with God extending his mercy to the Ninevites and learning, as Proverbs 24 instructs, not to 'gloat when your enemy falls'.

For us, the lesson is to accept that just as God's love and mercy meet us in our sinfulness, so they meet those who sin against us.

We cannot have one without the other and our challenge is to rejoice in the mercy that unites us all, regardless of, or perhaps because, we don't deserve it.

Breath prayer

Inhale: There is so much horror
Exhale: There is so much beauty

Week 34
Ordinary Time: Love rejoices with the truth

Reading: 2 John 1

> It has given me great joy to find some of your children walking in the truth, just as the Father commanded us.
> (v. 4)

It's often said that we live in a post-truth world. People can say whatever they want and claim it as truth by saying that it is *their* truth. But a truth based only on a single person's truth is experience, not truth.

The love that John talks about in this passage stands against post-truth and subjective truth, because Jesus is the embodiment of truth. Ethics writers Stassen and Gushee point out that not only was 'Jesus the embodiment of truth' but 'the Johannine community linked truth with Jesus and discipleship'.[33] It goes back to a key belief of John that I think we need to pay close attention to: that truthfulness is a matter of character. It's not just the absence of telling lies, but our commitment to integrity through all we say and do.

As John wrote, he was aware of the lies and distrust that false teachers were spreading among the early Church. He wanted to combat this by reorienting people to Jesus as the ultimate truth.

In our lives, false teachers might look like preachers in expensive sneakers, who tell us that the kingdom of God belongs to those with the shiniest Instagram grids, or that our faith can be measured by the size of our tithe. But the principle for responding to them is the same as it was for responding to false teachers in the first century. We can use Scripture and what we know of the character of Jesus to remind ourselves that love and truth cannot be separated.

It's beautiful that we're told love rejoices with the truth; it's not a stubborn acquiescence like my slow acceptance that I am not a machine that doesn't need rest (is that just me?). Love rejoices with the truth and values eternal truth over momentary happiness. The false teachers of today might appear different from those John warned of in the first century, but much like false teachers then, they stretch the truth of Jesus' teachings to make themselves sound plausible. In doing this they miss the vital point: the love we can rejoice in is the one that comes from the Father through the Son and by the Spirit. It's the commandment that we should love God, and each other, as we love ourselves. Anything that falls outside of this teaching falls outside of the boundary of God's truth. John talks about the antichrist. These false teachers are not just people who make doctrinal mistakes, but those who refuse to preach that Jesus is Lord, or insist that there are ways to God without love.

Sometimes it's easier to think that salvation can be reached simply by following the rules robotically, but the truth worth rejoicing in is that lawfulness without love isn't enough. In the same way, our relationships cannot flourish without love powering them. The truth cannot be full without love.

Prayer

Allow these verses from Psalm 25:1–5 to be your prayer today.

In you, LORD my God,
 I put my trust.

I trust in you;
 do not let me be put to shame,
 nor let my enemies triumph over me.
No one who hopes in you
 will ever be put to shame,

but shame will come on those
   who are treacherous without cause.

Show me your ways, Lord,
   teach me your paths.
Guide me in your truth and teach me,
   for you are God my Saviour,
   and my hope is in you all day long.

Week 35
Ordinary Time: Love always protects

Reading: Exodus 14

The LORD will fight for you; you need only to be still. (v. 14)

My son has a somewhat intense obsession with ancient Egypt. He has every (age-appropriate) book about the time, a pharaoh headdress, a Playmobil pyramid, and his most prized possession is a figure of Tutankhamun that his best friend brought back from a holiday to Cairo. Gone are the trains that dominated the first five years of his life. They have been replaced by an encyclopaedic knowledge of canopic jars, sarcophagi and the reign of Tutankhamun.

Before his devotion to all things ancient Egyptian, I have to admit that my own interest was somewhat limited to what we learn in the book of Exodus. I knew about mummification and pyramids, but most of my mental images came from the film *The Prince of Egypt*, and the part that always captivated me was when the Israelites were finally permitted to escape after the final plague killed the first-born Egyptian baby boys. It's a confusing and disturbing chapter of Scripture's story, in which God's loving protection comes at the cost of innocent blood – and not for the last time.

Because it was this final deadly plague that encouraged Pharaoh to free the Israelites after more than 400 years of slavery. God's people were free at last, but then we read about God hardening Pharaoh's heart, and he soon set off in pursuit of the slaves he had just released. Exodus 14:5 recounts Pharaoh's regret: 'What have we done? We have let the Israelites go and have lost their services!' It was this hardening of the heart that saw Pharaoh follow the Israelites. At this point, both sides would have assumed that the only possible outcome of a battle would be Israel's defeat, as they would be forced to run straight into the Red Sea. The Israelites complained to Moses (and not for the last time): 'Was it because there were no graves in Egypt that you brought us to the desert to die? What have you done to us by bringing us out of Egypt?' (v. 11).

From our perspective, we can marvel at how short their memory was, how quickly they forgot all that God had done to protect them. But without much reflection, I can recall times in my own life when I've acted similarly. It's all too easy to praise God in the short term for his protection, but then forget it all when we're faced with new dangers and challenges.

Despite this groaning and grumbling, God did go on to protect them in a mighty way. Moses encouraged the Israelites that they had God's protection, and all they needed to do was allow it. I remember as a young teenager, perhaps fourteen years old, being given these verses from Exodus 14 as I emerged from my first episode of depression. I had been striving to make myself better, but I was calmed by the knowledge that I needed only to be still. As Moses told the Israelites: 'Do not be afraid. Stand firm and you will see the deliverance the Lord will bring you today. The Egyptians you see today you will never see again. The Lord will fight for you; you need only to be still' (vv. 13–14).

For me then, and perhaps for the Israelites, the idea of being still was anathema. I thought I had to act to secure God's protection. Yet the Israelites and I were to learn that sometimes God's protection comes when we are simply still. Often it doesn't make logical sense that we are protected from some troubles but not all of them. I have wanted (and to be honest, I still want) to be protected from all the dangers that come my way. But in his love and wisdom, God does not wrap us in cotton wool. The Israelites' obstacle wasn't removed, even though God certainly could have removed the Red Sea. But a path was made through the trouble.

This is the love that always protects, not by removing all the trouble, but by making a way through it. In my own life, the way through has been with medication and counselling – not the Israelites' more dramatic pillars of wind and fire!

The love that protects empowers us to be still and trust in God when there seems to be no way through the pain. We can be a part of that for those we love too, by helping them to keep their eyes fixed on the Lord above rather than the trouble around.

Breath prayer

Inhale: God is our refuge
Exhale: Ever present in trouble

Week 36
Ordinary Time: Love always trusts

Reading: Proverbs 3:1–8

> Trust in the LORD with all your heart and lean not on your own understanding.
> (v. 5)

If you're familiar with the concept of a memory verse,[34] you've probably come across the above. These words are buried at the heart of the Christian faith, and promise that, by trusting in God, you will be led by God's wisdom, which will produce well-being.

Sometimes passages like this can feel glib amid the maelstrom of modern life. They can feel almost like a prosperity gospel-type promise that assures us of an easy life if only we follow God. But if we zoom out and look at the whole of Scripture, we get a bit more context. Jesus, who undoubtedly trusted in God with all his heart, and who never let love and faithfulness leave him (v. 3), did not live a life full of the peace and prosperity promised in verse 2.

I think this is probably more to do with our understanding of peace and prosperity than it is likely to be a biblical typo! We often consider peace and prosperity in strictly materialist terms – that there will be no wars and we'll have access to unlimited cash – but in the original Hebrew, the word we've translated as 'prosperity' can also mean 'flourishing' and 'well-being'.

Jesus was the Prince of peace, he experienced well-being and flourished in his life, even though, materially speaking, he wasn't wealthy. Jesus followed all of the wisdom this proverb expounds.

He did not forget God's law; love and faithfulness led him to lay down his life for his friends; he trusted and feared the Lord. And yet he was also called 'Man of Sorrows' and died as a criminal. These things do not sit in contrast with his wisdom but are the fruit of it. They are the reason we can always trust in God, because he does not ask us to do things he's not prepared to do himself. Jesus can be trusted to be our guide, because he's walked the steps of human life.

I'm not great at orientation or directions – mainly because I struggle to tell my left from my right unless I look for the hand where the index finger and thumb make the letter 'L'. It's not unreasonable for my husband to double check when I give him directions somewhere (and by 'double check' I mean look it up on Google Maps). In contrast, when my husband gives me directions, I trust him, because he's usually made the journey before and, at the very least, he knows how to read a map accurately. Our trust is based on our experience (of life and one another).

The same is true of our relationship with Jesus: we can trust him, because of what we know about how he loves us and how we know and love him. You might have a twenty-year faith you can fall back on, but it's not a prerequisite for trusting God. You can still look to Scripture and listen to the stories of others who worship Jesus.

Blessing

May we rest our weary hearts
In the arms of he who holds the world.

May we be steadied by he who calms the waves
As the tide ebbs and flows.

May we bask in the truth of our belovedness
As the sun shares its last beams.

Week 37
Ordinary Time: Love always hopes

Reading: Lamentations 3:19–24

Yet this I call to mind and therefore I have hope.
(v. 21)

In the middle of one of the most unrelenting and hopeless books in Scripture lies one of the most startling declarations of hope. It's the only part of Lamentations that is regularly quoted, because the rest of the text is full of raw honesty and pain. For example, the opening verses read: 'How deserted lies the city, once so full of people! How like a widow is she, who once was great among the nations!' (1:1).

And yet it is because of this backdrop of despair that these words – so full of hope – can be trusted. It's often easiest to follow God and remember we are loved, and believe that he is doing what's best for us, when life is going well and our prayers are being answered. But when life feels as if it's falling apart and everything seems to be going against us, believing in our belovedness is a lot more difficult.

If it's hard for us, it was definitely a struggle for the writer of Lamentations, who is sometimes thought to be Jeremiah, known as 'the weeping prophet'. It was definitely difficult for the whole of the exiled community, who were suffering far from home and far from the promises they believed God had given them.

The book is made up of five poems. It is at the mid-point of the central poem in Lamentations 3 that the writer speaks of God's loving-kindness, despite the loss and pain ruling their life. The author is remembering and recounting their pain and distress, but there is a turning point when they remember the love of God. Verses 21–23 proclaim: 'Yet this I call to mind and therefore I have hope. Because of the LORD's great love we are not consumed, for his compassions never fail. They are new every morning, great is your faithfulness.' These are perhaps some of the most famous words in Scripture, not least because they were the inspiration for the hymn 'Great is Thy Faithfulness', which, despite being written in 1923, is still sung in churches all over the world. Even so, we all too often forget that these words come from Scripture written in the hardest of times.

It's important to remember that hope isn't the same as optimism. It's not simply looking on the bright side. Love doesn't call for us to do that and be oblivious to the difficulties we face. It calls us not to an empty hope, but to put our hope in the person of Jesus.

There's a pattern here too, which is reflected in the Lord's Prayer, where we ask for what we need each and every day. The promises of compassion in Lamentations are 'new every morning'. And in the Lord's Prayer we ask for our daily bread. We don't get to stockpile hope, but neither do we have to beg for it; it's given to us as a gift when we choose to follow Christ.

Blessing

Sometimes hope is bold,
Unmistakeable and clear;
Other times it's fainter,
Harder to make out.
But hope does not
Rely on our recognition
But on its source:
The Father's power,
The Son's love,
The Spirit's companionship.
It is the only hope
That can propel us
To the promise
Of life lived in full.

Week 38
Ordinary Time: Love always perseveres

Reading: Hebrews 10:19–25

> Let us hold unswervingly to the hope we profess, for he who promised is faithful.
> (v. 23)

I can't say that perseverance is my favourite quality to practise. I certainly admire it in other people – those who run marathons or demonstrate endurance through some of what life has thrown at them. But in my own life, I don't love it. For one thing, it's really hard work. There have been times during the writing of this book that have required great perseverance – both in the writing and in life in general, like holding my ground when my little boy wants something he can't have. And let's not even get started on the perseverance required to finish a tax return.

Perseverance rarely relates to my favourite activities, but it is often related to love (with the exception of the tax return). It's love that demands and powers perseverance. Perseverance in faith is not a new thing. It's not restricted to the Church of the twenty-first century, but has been there since the very beginning of the faith.

In his letter to the Hebrews, Paul encourages his readers to persevere even when things are difficult; to hold fast to Jesus even when their belief is causing persecution and pain. And verse 23 tells us that 'he who promised is faithful'. What I find most encouraging and hopeful is that we aren't expected to persevere alone, by our own willpower and whatever inner strength we can muster. It's through Jesus and through being in a community with others. It's a reminder that we were never meant to do this life alone. We don't need a romantic partner in order to flourish, but we do need other people around us to help us bear the burdens we carry.

Jesus himself was surrounded by his disciples when he was on earth. But together, Father, Son and Spirit show us that relationship is a part of what it means for us to be made in the image of God. It means being in relationships. Perseverance can feel incredibly lonely. It can feel as if we are on life's treadmill with no room for anyone else. But while no one can live our lives and bear our suffering for us, they can be alongside and cheering us on.

One of my friends, Jade, was paralysed aged twelve and she is the picture of perseverance to me. I met her at Bible college and watched her do things that required a huge amount of energy and effort for her, when I would do them without thinking. But she would do those things with a patience and humour I admired hugely. She also drew on her faith in Jesus and the people around her. A few years ago, a crowdfunding campaign enabled her to get a new wheelchair to increase her independence and it's the perfect example of personal perseverance enhanced by the love of God and the love of other people.[35]

Perseverance doesn't get the best press, but it is powerful, and love makes it all the more so.

Blessing

'You're so brave!'
They exclaim.
And yet,
With each passing day,
You ache for a time
That does not require
Your bravery.
You are tired of courage,
The tension of expectation

To face each new challenge
Without fear, with fortitude.

God of gentleness,
May you meet us in our aching.
Father of compassion,
May you cover us with your peace.
Let us inhale our belovedness
And exhale our bravado.

Week 39
Ordinary Time: Love never fails

Reading: Romans 8:31–39

> In all these things we are more than conquerors through him who loved us.
> (v. 37)

This passage has been central to my life and faith for twenty years. When my faith grows cool or my hope is low, I return to these verses. They were the ones I held fast to in the depths of depression and whispered over my son when he was a newborn. When I didn't have the energy to read, I found I could rest in the truth of Paul's words that I'd memorised without even realising it.

As I write, the United Kingdom is swamped with campaigning for the 2024 election, and the vitriol and distrust often associated with political debate is rife. Every failure of the country is under the microscope and meanwhile there are wars raging in Ukraine, Gaza and countless other nations across the world. The scale of the heartbreak is too much to bear and it's difficult to summon hope when all around is despair.

There is an honesty in Paul's clear-eyed view of the world that comforts us even now. Our current situation is not so dissimilar to the division of the church in Rome. Paul talks of the 'hardship or persecution or famine or nakedness or danger or sword' in verse 35, and assures readers that even these greatest of troubles cannot keep us away from God's love.

We read a few weeks back that love rejoices in the truth, and that remains the same even when it is an uncomfortable or painful truth. Paul had spoken earlier in the chapter about all that was facing the church in Corinth and yet his response was not to deny the hardship but to remind and reaffirm us of the love that remains unfailing through it all.

That is our task too. We do not airbrush what is before us and around us, but we expand our vision to see the love of God that never fails us – the love of God shown most perfectly in the person and work of Jesus Christ. We don't pretend that it will result in a shiny, happy existence without pain or problems. Instead, we recognise that through it all we can rely on the love of God to sustain us through life's storms. We will fail one another, dream jobs will be lost, health problems will arise, families will disappoint and churches may splinter, but the love of God cannot and will not fail. It is the solid thing we can trust and hope in.

Over the past few years, the mental illness that I live with has raged through my life, leaving a trail of destruction in its wake. At one point, everything I valued and derived value from felt as if it were stripped away as my world shrunk to the four walls of my home. At my lowest and most lost, only two things remained real to me: the love I felt from those around me and the undeniable knowledge that God loved me. My mind had managed to twist most of what was good around me, but try as I might, I could not shift the knowledge and feeling that God was still there even when I felt failed by him. It didn't stop my questions or the feelings of abandonment, but it allowed my faith to remain.

I think the main reason for this was knowing that God's love didn't fail and this had nothing to do with me. It didn't matter that I couldn't perform the roles I held in my life or do the things that had always been constants in my faith, like attending church. All that mattered was knowing God didn't change and that the people around me were pointing to that unfailing love in every kindness they offered my family and me.

We will inevitably fail in loving one another. It's an unavoidable part of living in the world outside of Eden. But the love of God is as unshakeable and unfailing to us as it has been throughout the millennia, from the clothing of Adam and Eve when they had to leave Eden to the manna provided for the Israelites in the desert and God's persistent pursuit of his people, however far away they wandered. The good news of the gospel is that nothing separates us from God's unfailing love.

Let us end with a breath prayer to repeat throughout the week ahead whenever we need reminding.

Breath prayer

Inhale: Neither life nor death
Exhale: Can separate us from God's love

Week 40
Ordinary Time: Love is our shalom

Reading: John 10:1–13

> The thief comes only to steal and kill and destroy; I have come that they may have life, and have it to the full.
> (v. 10)

Everyone has mental health challenges – we know that better than any other generation in recent history. Even so, we can still find it difficult to know what to do when we're struggling with our mental health, whether that be due to life circumstances or mental illness. The world of mental health awareness can feel far removed from our faith, but in reality, while the phrase isn't seen in Scripture, the concept is weaved throughout the Bible and often summed up in the word 'shalom', which can be translated as 'wholeness', 'peace' or 'well-being'.

All too often, well-being can feel a million miles away. We find ourselves living with grief or experiencing parenting worries or we may have been diagnosed with a mental illness and find ourselves wondering where on earth God and his love are in it all. Life doesn't often look like we imagined, does it?

Sometimes, though, it's our imagination that has got the wrong end of the stick. When we read verses like John 10:10 above, we can have a tendency to imagine that Jesus is promising us a life without the thief that comes to steal and destroy. We think we're owed a life without fear or grief. But he's actually telling us that even though the thief will come (and mental illness has stolen a myriad of things from me), Jesus will remain and give us a life in spite of everything we face. In the passage, the sheep are not immune to the dangers around them, but the good shepherd is present and protective, and his familiar voice calls them home when they wander too far from him. So it is with us. The dangers and pain still surround us, but there is a voice we can learn to discern, and it calls our name. We are promised the presence and protection of the Good Shepherd, not the perfect life.

When Jesus promised a life to the full this side of a new creation, it included the parts of life and the emotions we would rather avoid. I'd probably have created an emotional life without anger or anxiety, sadness or shock, but that's not how things are and these emotions have functions. I trust – somewhat begrudgingly much of the time – that this is what fullness looks like, with our joy hidden inside our sorrow and love shown in its fullest through Jesus' arms stretched wide on the cross.

Shalom does not shy away from the sorrow. It encompasses it in a way that is almost impossible for us to understand.

Blessing

If today feels more like a burden than a blessing,
May we be reminded of his strength.
In the depths of our weakness,
If we're struggling to see life amid death,
May we be reminded of the truth planted in darkness.
If we're exhausted before the week begins,
May we be encouraged that God does not grow faint.
If we're struggling to see treasure in the darkness,
May we glimpse the joy nestled amid the sorrow.
If today feels like a step too terrifying,
May we remember you in the garden
And know we are not alone.

Week 41
Ordinary Time: Love shines through weakness

Reading: 2 Corinthians 4:1–18

> But we have this treasure in jars of clay to show that this all-surpassing power is from God and not from us.
> (v. 7)

When I've read this passage, in which Paul talks about treasure in jars of clay, I've always assumed the treasure was being hidden, because these were thick earthenware pots you could barely carry, let alone see through. I thought that the treasure was invisible when it was in the jars.

In actual fact these jars weren't sturdy pottery at all; they were poor-quality clay jars that might have been used as oil lamps. They were fragile enough to let the light shine through. These jars could not emit light on their own. They had to be filled – and so do we. The treasure in them could only be seen because of their weakness and frailty, and throughout the Bible we read examples of this. Whether it be Moses fearing God's call and enlisting Aaron to help him speak to Pharaoh, David's foolishness and cruelty when he sent Bathsheba's husband to his death, Peter's hot-headedness or Mary's busyness, it's through weakness that God's power and love shines the brightest.

This stands in stark contrast to the way things work in the world. We want to be the brightest and the best, and to show ourselves in the most flattering light. I certainly do if I'm taking a photo for my Instagram. But in the way of the upside-down kingdom, it is when we are at our weakest that we show God's power in the best way. As verse 7 tells us, it's 'to show that this all-surpassing power is from God and not from us'. When we are at our weakest, we show God's power all the more vibrantly, because it's proof that any power we're displaying isn't ours and can only come from heaven.

It's a reminder too that the Christian life is not a bed of roses. There is a school of thought that somehow being a Christian inoculates us against trouble and pain, but the truth is we are promised in John's Gospel that there will be trouble. Being a Christian isn't an easy option. It was hard in the first century when Paul was writing and living under Roman rule, and it still is hard today. But while the difficulties may be altogether different, the assurance of hope and power from the Lord remains as true now as it was then and it is rooted in our belovedness.

I'm not living the life I imagined I would – the original plan was that I'd be a missionary in Rwanda rather than a writer in the suburbs. I expect many of us would say the same; our childhood dreams don't often translate clearly into adult life (although some of us might be quite glad about that!). But there is joy and treasure in the life I lead now that I wouldn't have experienced if my life had gone to plan.

It is the times when I've found life the hardest that have glorified God the most. The mental illness that I live with pushes me to rely on God in ways that I probably wouldn't do otherwise. If I'm honest, I find myself on my knees in prayer more often when life gets difficult. Any gifts that God has graciously bestowed on me are best seen when I'm desperate.

When I started working for a charity, one of my first big jobs was to present at our national conference the findings of research we'd carried out. I'd been gearing up for it for months, as it involved talking about numbers, which is definitely not my strong point! However, in the weeks leading up to the conference, I became very unwell and had to be signed off work for a month. My carefully scheduled prep time disappeared. As frustrating and painful a time as it was, it meant that when I did the talk as a part of my phased return, I relied fully on the grace and strength of God to get me through. Like Paul, I could not boast in anything apart from the grace of Jesus Christ when the talk went well and I said the numbers in the correct order!

So next time you feel at your weakest, be reminded that it is now that God's strength shows itself in the boldest way.

Breath prayer

Inhale: God is our peace
Exhale: Even as the world rages on[36]

Week 42
Ordinary Time: World Mental Health Day

Reading: Genesis 32:22–32

> Then the man said, 'Let me go, for it is daybreak.' But Jacob replied, 'I will not let you go unless you bless me.'
> (v. 26)

My favourite example of God's strength being displayed in weakness is that of Jacob. We read his story in Genesis. He's one of the patriarchs, the heroes of the faith. And yet his story is one of deceit and running, of wrestling and ruining things. Despite this, God does what he does best and works in the brokenness.

Even from birth, Jacob was known as a deceiver. His name literally means 'he grasps the heel' – a Hebrew idiom for 'he deceives'. Can you imagine what it was like to grow up under that name, most loved by his mother, as Genesis tells us, but known as the second-best and a deceiver?

As is so often the case, Jacob's name became a kind of self-fulfilling prophecy. With the help of his mother Rebekah he deceived his brother Esau out of his blessing as the firstborn of the family. It was Jacob, not Esau, who received this blessing of 'heaven's dew and earth's richness – an abundance of grain and new wine', to be 'lord over [his] brothers' and 'those who curse you be cursed and those who bless you be blessed' (Genesis 27:28–29).

Jacob received this blessing, but it didn't work out as he might have hoped. He got the land and the family, but he was also forced to flee. He was conned by his father-in-law, who made him work for seven years to marry the love of his life, Rachel, only to be forced to marry her sister Leah. He then had to work another seven years to have the bride he wanted. Then as he prepared to meet Esau again, we find this curious episode when Jacob wrestled with God through the night.

I don't know if you've ever felt as if you were wrestling with God. Maybe you've wrestled with God about your children, your marriage, your singleness, your pain, your mental illness. I know I've wrestled with God over the completely contradictory demands of mental illness and motherhood. I've asked how I can be a good mum while engaging in the war for my mind; how I can be my best for my son while grappling with the debilitating side effects of medication and the belief that perhaps he would be better off without me. I've pushed back on God when contemplating the things I must do – in my case last year going into hospital for a short time – with the ache and fear of what my absence would do to my son.

I recorded the wrestle in my diary, and reading it back now I see an echo of Jacob's prayer in my own. Jacob cried, 'I will not let you go unless you bless me,' and I begged, 'I won't let you get away with abandoning me. You'd better make this okay. I can't do this without you.'

When nothing is certain and everything hurts, what was a comfort to me then and remains a comfort to me now is that through it all I am loved. Through the pain God loves me and won't leave me to face it alone. And the same is true for you too.

Prayer

Lord, we're weary
Of this wrestling,
The fighting
And the fear.

And yet we will not let go.

Lord, we're waiting
For the light,
The blessing
Of dawn.

And we will not let go.

Lord, there is wonder
In the ache
That remains,
That reminds,

That you don't let us go.

Week 43
Ordinary Time: Rebuilding

Reading: Haggai 1

> 'Is it a time for you yourselves to be living in your panelled houses, while this house remains a ruin?'
> (v. 4)

Often we can feel as though we're standing in the rubble. There has been so much loss and so much terror, it can seem as if all we are able to do is survey the wreckage. I'm weary. Are you?

Not being there with them, I can't say for certain, but I expect the Israelites felt something similar. A weariness and lack of motivation in a world that had changed beyond recognition. After years in exile, the Persians, who had replaced the Babylonians as captors, had allowed a remnant, led by Joshua and Zerubbabel, to return. It had been seventy years since they had last called Israel home. So they'd settled into their new/old home by building themselves new houses. But it was far from smooth sailing, as they were confronted with poverty and drought.

It's into this situation that Haggai brings his message, which challenges, comforts and inspires confidence in God's plan for humanity. First comes the challenge – because Haggai has some pretty strong words to say to the Israelites. They have procrastinated over building God's Temple, even though they've built their own homes. Verse 4 puts it pretty plainly: 'Is it a time for you yourselves to be living in your panelled houses while this house remains a ruin?' It goes further, saying that their living conditions aren't accidental; it's God's judgement upon them for putting him at the bottom of their priority list.

We can feel pretty uncomfortable hearing about judgement. It so often jars with what the gospels teach and how Jesus preached, but in the Old Testament God's judgement plays out as people experiencing consequences for their actions. I guess it's the cosmic equivalent of when my son was a toddler and he'd throw his toy off the side of our balcony and it would inevitably break and he couldn't use it any more. He had to live with the consequences of a broken bubble-maker and we had to live with the consequences of a rather sad toddler.

Haggai brings a challenge to the Israelites, but it's not the end of the story. Haggai's message is not just one of challenge; it's one of comfort. We didn't leave our son alone to cry over his broken toy; we comforted him, even though he wouldn't get back what he'd lost. Just as God doesn't leave us alone to live with the consequences of our actions.

Haggai is one of the few prophets whose words were heeded. In contrast, so many other prophets' words seemed to fall on unwilling ears. The Israelites listen to Haggai's words and the leaders Joshua and Zerubbabel get to work on rebuilding the Temple. But the results aren't what they expected. It doesn't live up to the former glory of Solomon's Temple and the Israelites are once again left discouraged. They wonder what God is doing.

C. S. Lewis describes God coming to rebuild your house but beginning to destroy it in a way you don't understand and seems to make little sense. You're confused and hurt until you realise he's not just building a little house for you, but a palace that he intends to share with you.[37]

This is God's grand plan for the restoration and redecoration of the world, and God offers his encouragement for the work. 'Take courage,' God says – not for the first time in Scripture. These words appear time and again in the Bible and, while the words can sometimes seem a little hollow when casually dropped into conversation, these are words of the King and Creator who also says, 'I am with you.'

We can face interior design disasters and disappointments. We can grieve what we've lost. But we can look forward in hope because our God not only tells us to take courage but promises, 'I am with you.' And this promise stretches from the rebuilding of the Temple to Jesus' final commissioning words and through the Spirit of God who breathes on us each day.

This promise is one we can be confident in; not because of external powers and politicians, but because God is someone we can trust. He's got a good track record and when we're faced with the impossible, we are reminded that we can trust in God's hope and love.

As minister and author Robert Fyall said: 'When we come to an apparent graveyard of our hopes, we need to renew our trust in a God who knows his way out of the grave.'[38] This is the God who made a way through the seas for his people to escape captivity, Jesus who walked on water and calmed storms, and who sent his Spirit to be with us always.

Breath prayer

Inhale: Take courage
Exhale: The Lord is sovereign over all

Week 44
Ordinary Time: Lavish love

Reading: 1 John 3:1–3; 4:17–21

> See what great love the Father has lavished on us, that we should be called children of God! And that is what we are! The reason the world does not know us is that it did not know him.
> (1 John 3:1)

The opening words of this passage are some of the most stunning words in Scripture about the love of God. The concept of the Father lavishing his love on us is one that is so far removed from the often staid view we have of God. I can be tempted to picture him as a strict dad standing and surveying the world with arms crossed in disapproval, but this picture of God is the dad who gets down on his knees with arms wide open to welcome his children to him.

There's a tone of near incredulity that God loves us so much he calls us his children. It's John saying, 'Look at this love we have,' calling our attention to it so that we don't miss it. We are not just subjects in the King's court – we're family.

This passage reminds us that the love of God is a gift. We did nothing to earn or deserve it. It's freely given. But it also serves as a reminder that the way we love one another should be governed by how God loves us. Our character and behaviour aren't separate from God's love. They are a response to it.

Beloved is where we begin, and loving is how we respond. Following the law and going against sin isn't something that should be done as a box-ticking exercise or even out of fear of the consequences of sin, but as an overflow of how God loves us.

It's still something I struggle with. Growing up I followed the rules, more because I was afraid of punishment than because I wanted to be loving (not that I actually recall any punishment other than the odd time out!). I was particularly proud of getting through secondary school without a detention (I was a little like the elder brother in the parable of the prodigal son!). But it wasn't primarily because I wanted my character to be pure or Jesus-like; it was because I was afraid of getting into trouble.[39] I can be the same now. I don't want to do the wrong thing, but often it's not about wanting to do the most loving thing, but rather doing the thing that won't get me into trouble. Perhaps you can relate to this?

In contrast, John is telling us that how we behave flows from what we believe about God's love for us. I wonder how our lives would change if each and every decision were made in a way that asked how we could best channel the love of God, rather than perhaps how we could get the best results or avoid trouble.

We are, first and foremost, God's children, so we can't serve God and sin at the same time. We will inevitably mess up and sin, that's for sure, but we are saved by Jesus' work on the cross. He enables us to continue as God's children when we have fallen short, because he took the burden of punishment.

Being loved by God doesn't give us a free pass to do what we want just because we are assured of his forgiveness. But it does allow us to return to him when we've done wrong, safe in the knowledge that it hasn't disrupted his love for us.

It echoes what John says later in his letter, in 1 John 4:18: 'There is no fear in love. But perfect love drives out fear, because fear has to do with punishment. The one who fears is not made perfect in love.' We want to be people whose belovedness encourages us to follow God's instructions out of love and a desire to be close to him, rather than following the rules like I did as a teenager out of fear of the consequences.

Breath prayer

Inhale: Whoever lives in love
Exhale: Lives in God and God in them

Week 45
Ordinary Time: Settling down

Reading: Jeremiah 29:1–14

> 'For I know the plans I have for you,' declares the Lord, 'plans to prosper you and not to harm you, plans to give you hope and a future.'
> (v. 11)

It's the verse that adorns a thousand bookmarks and notebooks. As I write, I have a photo frame with this verse engraved on it containing a picture of me at my baptism, aged thirteen. At that time this verse was written in countless cards to me from family and friends as I took that step of faith.

But, as beautiful as it is, the verse looks completely different when we read it in context. The preceding words tell God's people, exiled far from home with Jerusalem destroyed, that they are to build a life where they are. God tells them not to put life on hold until things look the way they are supposed to, because this is going to be their reality for a while to come – seventy years, in fact. Yes, God had a hope and future planned for them – but it wasn't necessarily going to look how they imagined it would.

When I was a teenage Christian in the early 2000s, I saw this verse as God telling me that he had big plans for me – that I was going to change the world. On the face of it, there's nothing wrong with aiming high and wanting to have a big, positive impact! But it's not a call for everyone to be at the forefront of changing culture. When I look at the Scriptures, I see countless characters doing 'big things' for God, but I see even more people doing small, even unremarkable, things in unremarkable places that are a part of the remarkable story of God. From rebuilding walls to crafting pottery, these works were no less valuable to the kingdom than the things that hit the headlines.

The work many of us are doing in our lives now can often feel insignificant and is certainly not done on any platform, from filing tax returns or stacking chairs on a Sunday, to raising children and simply getting through the day. We don't feel we're doing big things for God and sometimes we feel that we've failed our younger selves, who so longed for greatness. But I've felt a growing sense over the past few years that we need to stop glorifying the big things and rejoice in the small. The work of God is not measured by our metrics. The largest, glossiest churches are not holier than small village churches. The faithful work of God done the world over in a thousand small ways still proclaims his glory. We can change culture in the way we mentor the young people in our churches, raise our children, do business and volunteer. We can effect change in the way we resist the cry of 'more' to be content with less.

It's good to remind ourselves of the Beatitudes (Matthew 5:1–12), where we see the poor in spirit inhabit the kingdom of heaven and the meek inherit the earth. Some will do big things, and I pray we receive the grace and mercy to steward ourselves wisely, but all of us will do the small things: the meal rotas and the school drop-offs, the coffee rotas and the Sunday school. I want to be faithful with the small offering I have to give, and pray that it makes a difference to people.

I need to be reminded, and perhaps you do too, that God's work is in our weakness and lack, so that we might boast only in God's great love and mercy, available to all.

Prayer

The prayer below is based on the words of the Beatitudes found in Matthew 5:1–12 (*The Message*).

> Thank you for blessing us when we're at the end of our rope,
> So we may reflect more of you and your rule.

Thank you for blessing us when we've lost what is dear to us,
So we may be embraced by the one most dear to us.
Thank you for blessing us when we're content with who we are,
So we may be owners of all that can't be bought.
Thank you for blessing us when we have an appetite for you,
So we may enjoy the best of you.
Thank you for blessing us when we care for others,
So that we may feel ourselves cared for.
Thank you for blessing us when we get our hearts and minds right,
So we may see your work clearly in the world.
Thank you for blessing us when we make peace,
So that we can see our place in God's family.

Week 46
First Sunday of Advent: In the dark

Reading: Isaiah 9:1–7

> The people walking in darkness have seen a great light; on those living in the land of deep darkness a light has dawned. (v. 2)

You don't need me to tell you that it's dark. It's a dark world and it feels as though we are living in dark times. I will not recount the contours of the darkness here; we each have our own to bear, as well as those we share – the very weight of this wonderful and broken world we live in.

And where is God in it all? Where is he in the war, the slaughter of innocents, the mental illnesses, the climate emergency; the days when our heartbreak is too heavy to bear?

I believe that Advent, perhaps more than any other time in the church year, speaks to us in the dark. Even in our darkness, in the shadows of death, the light will come, but it is not light here yet. It was true then because Jesus had not yet come to earth; it's true now because he has not yet returned and the world has not been made new. Perhaps we, like the Israelites, are living in the shadows. We know the light is there, but we can't quite step into it.

Advent admits this reality; it doesn't shy away from the shadows but rather recognises them. In the words of Fleming Rutledge:

> Advent is the season that, when properly understood, does not flinch from the darkness that stalks us all in this world.

> Advent begins in the dark and moves toward the light – but the season should not move too quickly or too glibly, lest we fail to acknowledge the depth of the darkness.[40]

It's so tempting to avoid the darkness, isn't it? Perhaps we fear it so much because we have failed to allow it the place in creation that God carved out for it. It's worth noting that when God said, 'Let there be light,' in Genesis 1:3 and called it good, he didn't need to leave a space for the darkness in the creation he called good. And yet it remains and it is not left without purpose, adorned by the beauty of the stars so casually crafted: 'He also made the stars' (v. 16).

Perhaps it is for us to accept that the darkness is not black and white. It can undeniably be a place of fear and loss, but so too it can be a place of growth and wonder, of lessons that can be learned no other way. We do not learn these lessons alone. It is dark, but just as a small child is comforted in their fear of the darkness when someone joins them, so too are we joined in our fear and discomfort.

The oft-quoted names of the Messiah are not just titles; they are descriptions of the one we both wait for and hold close in Advent. Verse 6 declares that 'he will be called Wonderful Counsellor, Mighty God, Everlasting Father, Prince of Peace'. Those hearing Isaiah's words would have recognised that these were not just names of a new king but names of the Messiah. He would be the one they had been waiting for and he was the reason we need not fear the darkness of the unknown. He is the one we are waiting for and is everything we could hope for.

As we light the flicker of the first Advent candle, let us be reminded that the darkness around it makes it all the more beautiful. The faintest hope that despair will not extinguish it. The God who created the light of day to go alongside the darkest of nights will grant us the wisdom to recognise the treasures in the darkness – even if we still hope for dawn.

Blessing

Come, Emmanuel.

Remind us of the work
Only the dark can do
In the deepest places.

Come, Emmanuel.

Remind us that you too
Have tasted womb and tomb
And yet risen in glory.

Come, Emmanuel.

Ever 'God with us',
Ever Prince of Peace,
Ever Wonderful Counsellor,
Ever Mighty God,
Everlasting Father.

As we remain beloved
On the darkest nights
As on the brightest of days.

Week 47
Second Sunday of Advent: Facing the dark

Reading: Genesis 1:1–18

> God saw that the light was good, and he separated the light from the darkness.
> (v. 4)

As we established last week, now more than ever before we do not like to accept darkness in our lives, especially in the run-up to Christmas. We don't like to face it, and we don't have to face it. We can turn on the lights as soon as we enter a room, stick to roads with street lights and most of us carry a phone that can act as a torch wherever we go. But the truth is, darkness was not banished at creation; it was given boundaries.

The story of Advent is one in which we cannot escape the dark realities of human life. The dark times range from those days under Roman rule when Mary and Joseph were forced to travel to Bethlehem, to these days of war, political unrest and whatever personal and communal pain we are facing. The very human life that God himself would inhabit through Jesus. It also tells us the story of what is to come; that when Jesus returns to make all things new it will not be in a virgin's womb but amid pain and in power (Luke 21:27).

I find Advent comforting because of this. It doesn't shy away from the realities of this world – it refuses to blind us to the pains of this world and our lives with fairy lights. Instead it shows us another way. It seems to me that God was well aware that we need the darkness as much as we need the light. It's true for all of creation. Life cannot be grown or sustained without the darkness. In the words of Barbara Brown Taylor, which I quote far too often: 'New life starts in the dark. Whether it is a seed in the ground, a baby in the womb, or Jesus in the tomb, it starts in the dark.'[41]

There will be times when we rail against it, when the shadows are full of grief and trauma that we simply cannot bear, but there are also times when our eyes grow accustomed to the dark and we begin to see things we could never see in the glow or the glare. All too often when we fear the dark, it is because we fear the unknown rather than the darkness itself. Advent invites us to accept the darkness as a place of rest, growth or wrestling. And in our acceptance of the darkness, I wonder if we are echoing Mary's own acceptance of her calling.

Mary's response to the news that she was carrying the King of kings in her womb was not one of uncomplicated delight. She was greatly troubled by the angel's appearance. But her acceptance gave way to our own: that inviting Jesus in will not mean a trouble-free life, but it will welcome us into the cosmic mystery of irresistible grace.

Our acceptance may be easy or more of a wrestle. Mine has been both at various points in my life, but it is an acceptance I will never regret, because I would rather have Jesus in the dark than be alone in the light.

Blessing

As wars rage
And our pain
Rumbles on,
We find ourselves
Immune to festivities.

We're attuned
To the ache
In ancient stories,

The poverty,
The murderous rule,
Refugees far from home.

And perhaps if
The ache has echoed
Through the generations,
So too will the comfort
Born as a babe:
Our Emmanuel.

Week 48
Third Sunday of Advent: Journey to the light

Reading: Luke 1:45–53

And Mary said: 'My soul glorifies the Lord.'
(v. 46)

'Are we nearly there yet?' These are words that anyone who has shared a journey with a young child will be familiar with (regardless of the length of the journey). But at this point in Advent we do seem to turn a corner. We have acknowledged the darkness we face, but it has almost felt premature before now to think about the light that is coming. This is the light promised in Jesus and the light we are promised with his return.

All journeys have these turning points at which we know where we're headed and we begin to see signs of home. For me, it's usually South Mimms services that signals home isn't too far off. We don't know the time and the place when we will see the world made new, when there will be no more tears or crying or pain. But there is something in this week's lectionary readings that points us directly to Jesus' coming. The light of the world was coming. It would step into our darkness so that we'd never have to face it alone again.

It's seen in the extraordinary words of the Magnificat, Mary's song and prayer recorded in Luke and which Bonhoeffer called 'the most passionate, the wildest, one might even say the most revolutionary hymn ever sung.'[42] For me, it's not just the contents that make it astonishing. It's that it's sung by a girl no older than fourteen, who has just been told that she, a virgin, would give birth to the Son of God.

When I was ten, I played Mary in the school nativity and my version of Mary's response to the news was a song that declared, 'Lord, as you've spoken, let it be; may your will be shown in me.' I recall even then thinking that I would have so many more questions and that Mary's acceptance and faith was far greater than my own.

But Mary's response to the news that she was carrying the Son of God wasn't one of simple acquiescence. Other verses tell us that she was greatly troubled by the news. She wrestled with the revelation, yet still said yes. It makes it even more mesmerising for me that her wrestle led her closer to God.

Our wrestles with God and his plans for us aren't just acceptable; they are perhaps the very preparation we need for the journey ahead of us. Whether it be Moses questioning his ability, Jacob's wrestle in the dark, Mary's troubled thoughts about her calling or Jesus' own blood-soaked prayers, we are shown that we have a God who recognises the cost of calling.

Most extraordinary about Mary's journey, however, is not the wrestle, but the proclamation that follows it. The Magnificat is not just about the journey she was embarking on, but the journey the Lord was on as he continued to draw his people closer to him. Luke 1:50–52 says: 'His mercy extends to those who fear him, from generation to generation. He has performed mighty deeds with his arm; he has scattered those who are proud in their inmost thoughts. He has brought down rulers from their thrones but has lifted up the humble.'

Mary spoke of the kind of person Jesus would be in his subversive mercy that would reach people beyond those expected to the ordinary people like her, who didn't have fanfare but had faith.

As Amy Orr-Ewing says in her book *Mary's Voice*: 'To the lowly, the oppressed, the abused, the vulnerable and the powerless, Mary's song is a cry of hope.'[43] Her song is needed now just as much as it was then – in a world that feels ever darker, where those with power wield it with violence and the innocent are left to fend for themselves. We can be reminded that Jesus brought hope and power not just for those he met 2,000 or so years ago, but for us too in all our own weaknesses and fears. And he did it not through violence and fear, but through the obedience and prophetic prayers of a teenage girl who would become the mother of God and remain by his side from the cradle to the cross.

Breath prayer

Inhale: His mercy extends
Exhale: From generation to generation

Week 49

Fourth Sunday of Advent: Light breaking through

Reading: Luke 1:39–45

> 'Blessed is she who has believed that the Lord would fulfil his promises to her!'
> (v. 45)

I'm writing this on the longest night of the year; the hours of darkness win today. It may be the most painful and protracted night, but it signals something else: that light is going to grow.

There is a similar point in the birth of anything. When things are at their darkest and most painful, there is a breakthrough, whether it be the birth of a baby, the final stages of adoption, the darkness of the cocoon that holds the butterfly from breaking out, the therapy session that breaks your heart but begins the journey to clearing your mind, the last push on the project you've poured your heart and soul into. We cannot birth anything without breakthrough – without breaking. It hurts. And it hurts no less because of what will follow, because what follows is an unknown.

The child, however he or she comes, will be their own person, and however parenting looks for you it will break your heart and bring you joy. It was true for both Mary and Elizabeth when they met in the midst of their miraculous pregnancies, one far past child-bearing age and the other a virgin. Both carried babies they would love and nurture before sending them to lives of unthinkable difficulty and tragedy. Pregnancy itself is a liminal space. Psychologist Joan Raphael-Leff says: 'On a deep unconscious level, the pregnant woman hovers between internal and external worlds, at a crossroads of past, present and future; self and other.'[44] For Mary and Elizabeth, this was perhaps truer than it had ever been and ever would be again.

Crossroads, however joy-filled they may be, are also painful. They wrench us from the familiar into the unknown. And regardless of whether you've experienced parenthood or pregnancy, you will doubtless know this to be true. I feel it each time I press 'publish' or submit a manuscript – these words that have been mine alone become public property, ready to be peered at, critiqued and challenged. I felt it acutely when I left the charity I founded to step into an imagined but as yet unconfirmed future. We feel it when we see what God has done and try to imagine what a re-created world might mean.

Joseph too stepped into the unknown when he waited alongside his community for the Messiah. He accepted the angel's words, risking the shame of being with a woman who was pregnant outside of marriage, journeyed alongside Mary and understood that this baby who was not his would be 'God with us' for everyone. It was Joseph who was told that this child would be Emmanuel. The birth of this child was the breaking of everything he had ever known, something Madeleine L'Engle put so beautifully in her poem 'O Sapientia':

> It was from Joseph first I learned
> of love. Like me he was dismayed.
> How easily he could have turned
> me from his house; but, unafraid,
> he put me not away from him
> (O God-sent angel, pray for him).
> Thus through his love was Love obeyed.[45]

The light of the world is drawing near. It is a light that will illuminate everything – the beauty and brutality of birth, the futility of war – and it will come to each of us in the whisper of dawn that God is with us. Emmanuel for each and every one of us.

Blessing

It is the mystery
Behind the merriment.
It is the hush
As the curtain rises,
The wait
Before the fulfilment,
The tears
Before the comfort.
It is the dark
Before the dawn.
Advent is the grief
Before the morning joy,
And morning is coming.

Week 50
Christmas: The light shows us what God is like

Reading: John 1

> The Word became flesh and made his dwelling among us. We have seen his glory, the glory of the one and only Son, who came from the Father, full of grace and truth.
> (v. 14)

The first time I heard preaching on John chapter 1 it changed my life and my faith for ever. I told this story in my first book, *Learning to Breathe*, but I think it's worth repeating here.

I was drowning in depression, I'd taken an overdose mere weeks before and that morning, as a church, we were reeling from the news that a young mother had died, suddenly and unexpectedly. I remember thinking for the first time that perhaps the Christmas story I'd known all of my life didn't cut it in the real world. I didn't know how the baby in a manger, the shepherds and the wise men were relevant to my pain and our church's grief. But into my cynicism and hard-heartedness, a word was preached that I've never forgotten. I listened to the recording of it so many times that even now I can recite it word for word. The opening lines were: 'The Christian faith is utterly useless … if it can't help us to know what God is like and how God can be known. The Christian faith is utterly useless … if what it says about God says nothing whatsoever to the real world of people: for our living and for our dying – especially when life should deal the most dreadful and cruellest of blows.'[46]

The words allowed me to see that my faith was in something stronger than I'd perhaps believed. The God in whom I'd entrusted my life could handle it, and the journey of faith was worth the fight because Jesus left heaven's glory for earth's pain because of God's love for us.

Christmas is useless if it's a story about a rotund man giving out presents. But if it's a story of the King of heaven and earth coming to earth for our sake, who was there from the beginning and with us to the very end of the age, then Christmas means everything in our hurting and our hoping, our loving and our lovelessness.

Christmas means everything if Jesus shows us what God is like. It means that we are loved and free, and he is with us through whatever life throws our way. It means that as much as I enjoy a colour-coordinated Christmas tree and decorations, this means nothing in the light of heaven's child becoming human. He tasted every flavour of human life so that we never have to face the trials and turbulence of life alone.

This is where we begin: beloved and never alone. It's the story that every facet of the nativity repeats; that Jesus came to us because God so loved the world. John's Gospel talks about the Word becoming flesh and dwelling among us. This doesn't mean that Jesus came to be a casual observer of humanity, but that he came to get stuck into what it means to be human, in the joy, the sorrow and everything in between. The Greek text can be translated as 'he pitched his tent among us'. It's the Son of God getting involved in the realities of life, even when they're difficult and messy (my only experience of camping and pitching a tent was both).

The willingness of Jesus to leave heaven's splendour for the humility of earth is the greatest sign of love ever shown. It's the reason Jesus can offer us comfort; not just because he came to earth, but because he shows us what God is like. John writes: 'No one has ever seen God, but the one and only Son, who is himself God and is in the closest relationship with the Father, has made him known.' (v. 18). We can know what God is like by getting to know Jesus, and Jesus shows us throughout Scripture that he is the personification of loving-kindness, ready to reach out to those most in need.

Christmas, contrary to the suggestion of most greetings cards, isn't a time for universal happiness. It is the unquenchable hope that relies not on our circumstances but Christ making himself known and drawing close.

Blessing

It's okay if your Christmas wasn't picture perfect.
It's okay if the pictures were perfect but you weren't okay.
The day may be over, but the season has just begun.
It's not about the presents, the lights – even the carols.
It's about the Mighty God who became flesh.
It's about the Everlasting Father with the deepest love.
It's about the Prince of Peace, who reigns even now.
It's about the Wonderful Counsellor, closer than we know.
Our God is with us; in our peace and our pain
As the wars rage and terrors tremble.
Our God is with us, his love, peace, hope and joy,
So that we may share them with others far and near;
That we may share his joy amid despondency,
Peace in conflict,
Love where there is hate
And hope where there is hopelessness.
God with us – it's sometimes all we have
And yet it is more than we can ever ask or imagine.

Week 51
Sunday after Christmas: Glory around

Reading: Luke 2:8–20

> An angel of the Lord appeared to them, and the glory of the Lord shone around them, and they were terrified.
> (v. 9)

The terror and fear of the shepherds is a part of the nativity story we tend to miss against the backdrop of the traditional scene. And yet as I was thinking about it today, I remembered that my son's line in his Reception nativity play as Shepherd Number 3 was, 'Let's get out of here!' The coming of Christ didn't look how the first-century Jews expected it to. It didn't look how we think it ought to have done. Even though I've read the story more times than I can count, I forget that the story of the shepherds wasn't just them gazing beatifically at the infant in the manger. It was an encounter that began with great fear. Verse 9 tells us that 'they were terrified'.

The glory of God that was on display across the skies as angels filled the horizon was scary. The glory of God is more than our humanity can manage. As Timothy Keller says: 'When God's glory appears, it always accentuates and intensifies our fundamental fearfulness because we are alienated from God.'[47]

Keller's words ring true, don't they? When I think about the times in Scripture when God's glory shows up, people are frightened. When Moses asked to see God's glory he could not see his face. Isaiah 6 depicts the glory of God making the earth shake and smoke appear everywhere. In 1 Kings 8:11 we read that 'the priests could not perform their service because of the cloud, for the glory of the LORD filled his temple'.

The same is true for the shepherds. The glory of God was so intense and pure, it shone so brightly in the skies, it must have made the gap between them and God feel bigger than ever. This glory was not reserved for anyone outwardly impressive or royal, but for shepherds. Shepherds weren't of a high social class, even though they were probably priests caring for animals that would be sacrificed, which is perhaps another sign that's often overlooked.

When the shepherds encountered the full glory of God, the angel didn't tell them to hide or look away, as God had done before. He said, 'Do not be afraid. I bring you good news that will cause great joy for all the people' (v. 10). Through Jesus, the glory of God had come to earth in perhaps the least glorious way. The shepherds were encouraged to get up close to the baby Jesus. With the incarnation of Jesus, the Word becoming flesh, they were brought closer to the glory of God than ever before. As it says in John 1:14, 'The Word became flesh and made his dwelling among us. We have seen his glory, the glory of the one and only Son, who came from the Father, full of grace and truth.'

When God sent Jesus to earth, he shared his glory in the most intimate way since Eden. The shepherds saw the glory, but they also got close to the glory of Jesus, as Mary and Joseph had before them and as Peter, James and John would at the transfiguration. The glory and the grace of Jesus sit at the heart of who he is and represent the lengths to which God went in order to prove he loves us, by sending his Son from glory to obscurity.

Breath prayer

Inhale: Blessed is the King
Exhale: Who comes in the name of the Lord

Week 52

Second Sunday after Christmas: Feast of the Holy Innocents

Reading: Matthew 2:13–18

> A voice is heard in Ramah, weeping and great mourning,
> Rachel weeping for her children and refusing to be comforted,
> because they are no more.
> (v. 18)

The Feast of the Holy Innocents, which remembers Herod's slaughter of Hebrew baby boys in his murderous campaign to kill the infant Jesus, doesn't fit particularly easily into a Christmas sermon series. There is a temptation to skip over it altogether, to move from the shepherds to the wise men without mentioning the massacre. But to do this is a disservice not only to Scripture but to those who are still living this story of losing all they have and being forced to flee their homelands.

Power still corrupts; there are leaders today who would rather see innocent blood shed than relinquish control of borders or nations. We see it in smaller ways too, when people would rather cling to power than seek reconciliation. We are probably all guilty of it at times.

This story's place in the Christmas narrative, although uncomfortable, is vital. We cannot turn away from suffering and sin in favour of fairy lights. As theologian Fleming Rutledge said so powerfully:

> The Christmas story is anchored to our lives and to the wickedness of this world by the grief of Rachel …The authors of

> scripture did not turn away from the unimaginable suffering of children. God the Father did not turn away. Jesus did not turn away.[48]

The inclusion of this story encompasses all of humanity in the story of Christmas; it's a reminder that we need not paint on a smile and pretend that everything is okay in order to come to Jesus. It's a reminder that the world is still far from Eden and that we live in a world with war and terror. But even so, we remain beloved. Our pain does not exclude us from God's story or God's love.

As I write in 2024, wars are still raging, children are still suffering and refugees are still losing their lives in their quest for safety. Those things that were painful realities in the first century remain for us in the twenty-first century. But more importantly, not only is God still present and active in the midst of it, he is still worthy of the praise and worship of heaven and earth.

Remembering the slaughter of those Hebrew baby boys all those millennia ago forces us to remember all those slaughtered today. The loss endured by the Hebrew people mirrors the loss that millions face today. Marking the Feast of the Holy Innocents is a way to be reminded that the God who crafted the earth cares deeply and loves furiously each life lost and all those left behind who are forced to live with fathomless grief.

Blessing for the Feast of the Holy Innocents

It's a day we don't want
Amid the sparkle,
The rejoicing, the reunions.

'A voice is heard in Ramah,
Weeping and great mourning,
Rachel weeping for her children
And refusing to be comforted,
Because they are no more.'

And yet we must,
For Rachel is not alone.
Today thousands of mothers
Are weeping for children lost to them.

Between the virgin birth
And the sages guided by the stars
Lies the ancient story
Of Herod's slaughter.

Thousands of baby boys
Killed to extinguish
The light of the world
As he joined the refugees.

Afterword

It feels somewhat poetic that I am writing this epilogue as the hush of Advent begins. I started writing this book during a damp and dreary spring. Now the waiting and hoping feels heavy in the air as we end a year of turmoil – both politically for us all and personally for me.

While I was knee-deep in writing about the facets of God's almighty love, I was undergoing electroconvulsive treatment (ECT) for the depression that has haunted my life for twenty years. I wrote in between treatments and, somewhat surreally, I found myself editing chapters that I could barely recall writing. Short-term memory loss is a common side effect of ECT and it turns out that much of what was lost in the library of my memory was my own writing. It was strange, but it was also a great mercy, because as I re-read the Scriptures that so beautifully explore the breadth and depth of God's love, I was astounded by their truth once again.

It doesn't take ECT for us to forget or become immune to the love of God. It happens as life rushes by and we are consumed by the work that must be done, the bills that must be paid and the children we're entrusted to raise. It is all too easy to miss the majesty of God's coming to earth as a vulnerable human baby, especially if it's a story we have been familiar with for many years.

It is my hope that, as you have journeyed through the year, you have heard the voice of God call you beloved. It might be the first time you've heard yourself called beloved, or it might be that you're hearing it again after life and pain have shouted louder names. However you find yourself, I pray that you will allow 'beloved' as an identity to root itself deeply into your heart.

In the Bible there is a story of Jesus watching people bring their financial offerings to the Temple. Rich men casually toss large amounts of money in without a second thought, and then a widow drops in two gold coins. Jesus tells his disciples, 'Truly I tell you, this poor widow has put more into the treasury than all the others. They all gave out of their wealth, but she, out of her poverty, put in everything – all she had to live on' (Mark 12:43–44). It is a reminder, I believe, that it is not the value of what we give that matters to Jesus; it is how we love him with that offering.

The knowledge of how we are loved by God is where all of our thoughts and actions should flow from. It's not easy, but it's the call central to what Jesus says is the greatest commandment – that we should love God, love ourselves and love one another.

Beloved is where we begin, and loving is how we move through life in all its fullness.

Acknowledgements

It has been a somewhat rocky road getting this book into your hands and I could not have done it without the incredible people supporting me!

Immeasurable thanks are due:

To my husband Phil, for being unfailingly supportive of my work, writing and life in all its ups and downs.

To my wonderful Mummy, for being my greatest cheerleader since the very beginning.

To my family; Dad, Gini and the whole Newham clan for your support and love.

To my friends old and new for their companionship, texts, humour and support over the past few years – with a special shout out to Abby, my working-from-home buddy whose company on Monday mornings has helped this book immensely!

To Simon, for all the encouragement, support and mentoring you've given me for more than twenty years.

To John Buckeridge, for reading the first chapters of this book and being so encouraging.

To the staff at The Orchards, whose kindness has helped me in ways they will probably never know.

To the team at SPCK; from Elizabeth Neep, who helped me nurture the first idea of this book, Lauren Windle for her wise and wonderful editing and those in between, Margaret, Rio, Emily and everyone else involved in getting this book into your hands with such a glorious cover!

And finally, to all those who have read and supported my writing with such love and encouragement – I hope you enjoy this one.

Notes

1 Richardson, J., *Circle of Grace: A book of blessings for the seasons* (Orlando, FL: Wanton Gospeller Press, 2015), Kindle edn, p. 84.

2 Alderman, L., 2016: https://www.nytimes.com/2016/11/09/well/mind/breathe-exhale-repeat-the-benefits-of-controlled-breathing.html (accessed 25/9/24).

3 Keller, T., *Hidden Christmas: The hidden truth behind the birth of Christ* (London: Hodder Faith, 2016), p. 64.

4 Hare, Douglas R. A., *Matthew: Interpretation: A Bible commentary for teaching and preaching* (Louisville, KY: Westminster/John Knox Press, 2009), p. 21.

5 Held Evans, Rachel, *Searching for Sunday: Loving, leaving, and finding the Church* (Nashville, TN: Thomas Nelson, 2015), Kindle edn, p. 156.

6 Craddock, F., *Luke: Interpretation: A Bible commentary for teaching and preaching* (Louisville, KY: John Knox Press), p. 40.

7 Peabody, J., 2021: https://www.christianitytoday.com/ct/2021/december-web-only/advent-waiting-for-jesus-lessons-from-simeon-anna.html (accessed 5/8/2024).

8 Harper, Lisa Sharon, *The Very Good Gospel: How everything wrong can be made right* (New York: Random House Inc., 2016), Kindle edn, p. 31.

9 Manning, Brennan, *Abba's Child: The cry of the heart for intimate belonging* (Colorado Springs: NavPress, 2015), p. 42.

10 Duncan Smith, Stephanie, *Even After Everything* (New York: Convergent Books, 2024).

11 See: https://www.instagram.com/p/C3YLhDurDOd/?igsh=MW05YWZneW1yMWN5dA== (accessed 25/9/24).

12 Peterson, Eugene H., *Lights a Lovely Mile: Collected sermons of the church year* (Colorado: Waterbrook, 2023).

13 Ponsonby, Simon, *Amazed by Jesus* (Edinburgh: Muddy Pearl, 2020).
14 Storkey, Elaine, *Women in a Patriarchal World: Twenty-five empowering stories from the Bible* (London: SPCK, 2020), p. 91.
15 Nikondeha, K., *Defiant: What the women of Exodus teach us about freedom* (Grand Rapids, MI: William B. Eerdmans Publishing Company, 2020), p. 43.
16 Arthur Riley, Cole, *This Here Flesh: Spirituality, liberation and the stories that make us* (London: John Murray Press, 2022).
17 Wolterstorff, Nicholas, *Lament for a Son* (Grand Rapids, MI: William B. Eerdmans, 1996), p. 26.
18 Pope Benedict XVI, *Jesus of Nazareth: From the entrance into Jerusalem to the resurrection* (London: Catholic Truth Society, 2011), p. 4.
19 Newham, Rachael, *And Yet: Finding joy in lament* (London: SPCK, 2020), Kindle edn, pp. 88–9).
20 Haidt, Jonathan, *The Anxious Generation: How the great rewiring of childhood is causing an epidemic of mental illness* (London: Penguin Books, 2024).
21 Keller, T., *King's Cross: Understanding the life and death of the Son of God* (London: Hodder & Stoughton, 2013).
22 For the whole poem see, for example: https://thejesusquestion.org/2013/10/28/jesus-of-the-scars-by-edward-shillito/ (accessed 21/01/25).
23 Wolterstorff, *Lament for a Son.*
24 Brown, Brené, *The Gifts of Imperfection: Let go of who you think you're supposed to be and embrace who you are* (Danvers, MA: Hazelden Publishing, 2018).
25 Bessey, Sarah, *Field Notes for the Wilderness: Practices for an evolving faith* (London: SPCK, 2024).
26 See: https://www.glennpackiam.com/post/what-does-the-ascension-of-jesus-mean (accessed 25/09/2024).
27 Sproul, R. C., *John: An expositional commentary* (Orlando, FL: Legonier Ministries, 2019).
28 Church of England, 'Prayers for starting every day with God': https://www.churchofengland.org/faith-life/everyday-faith/everyday-prayers#na (accessed 21/01/25).

29 This quote is commonly misattributed to C. S. Lewis, but it's generally believed that Pastor Rick Warren said this in one of his talks.

30 Available at: https://www.psychologytoday.com/gb/blog/the-wisdom-of-anger/202303/the-wisdom-of-aristotle-on-anger-management (accessed 15/08/2024).

31 Card, M., *Inexpressible: Hesed and the mystery of God's lovingkindness* (Lisle, IL: InterVarsity Press, 2018), p. 36.

32 See: https://www.britannica.com/topic/schadenfreude (accessed 29/07/2024).

33 Gushee, David P. and Glen H. Stassen, *Kingdom Ethics: Following Jesus in contemporary context* (Grand Rapids, MI: William B. Eerdmans, 2003), p. 377.

34 For those unfamiliar with memory verses, they're short Bible verses often given to children to remember, reflect on and recite over a holiday club or kids' church sessions. There is usually some kind of sweet treat as a prize/incentive.

35 You can read Jade Reynolds' story in the book she co-authored with her husband John, *Able to Laugh* (London: SPCK, 2024).

36 Adapted from the words of Kate Bowler and Jessica Richie, *Good Enough: 40ish devotionals for a life of imperfection* (London: Ebury Publishing, 2022).

37 C. S. Lewis, *Mere Christianity* (New York: Macmillan Co., 1960), p. 160.

38 Fyall, Robert, *The Message of Ezra & Haggai: Building for God* (London: IVP, 2010).

39 To this day I'm still not entirely sure why I was so terrified of the idea of a detention, but in my mind it was a punishment of mythical proportions!

40 Rutledge, Fleming, *Means of Grace: A year of weekly devotions* (Grand Rapids, MI: William B. Eerdmans, 2021).

41 Brown Taylor, B., *Learning to Walk in the Dark* (London: Canterbury Press, 2014), p. 129.

42 Bonhoeffer, D. (ed. and trans. E. H. Robertson), *Dietrich Bonhoeffer's Christmas Sermons* (Grand Rapids, MI: Zondervan, 2005).

43 Orr-Ewing, A., *Mary's Voice: Advent reflections to contemplate the coming of Christ* (London: Worthy, 2023), p. 80.

44 Raphael-Leff, Joan, in Lucy Jones, *Matrescence: On the metamorphosis of pregnancy, childbirth and motherhood* (London: Penguin Books, 2023), p. 38.
45 L'Engle, M., *Miracle on 10th Street: And other Christmas writings* (New York: Random House Publishing Group, 2019), p. 98.
46 Sermon given by the Revd Simon Smith, 'Christmas in the real world'. Used by permission.
47 Keller, *Hidden Christmas*, p. 113.
48 Rutledge, *Means of Grace*, p. 27.